MAUREEN DOUGHERTY

WOMEN

Blurring Books

In Maureen Dougherty's paintings, a curious medley of variegated characters spills out pell mell, unfiltered, almost seeming to bypass the author's second thoughts or better judgments. Thankfully so. Much of contemporary life consists of fending off new manipulative inroads. Everything seems to be trying to do a number on us, astonish us, control us. Dougherty is aware of the inherent provocativeness of her figures, but they simply appear, they aren't forced on us. Neither are they faux naïf, faux sophisticated, faux artful. They are strange but put forth without overriding attitude. Honest and yes, trusting. Guileless fantasies transformed into tableaus of colorful personalities, filmic fragments, salacious scenes.

Evidence of her past years as an abstract painter are in the lively yet purposeful, painted paint. Imagery arrives via the material substance without flourish or mannerism. Note that her sources derive from both inside and outside painting culture. One can identify tropes and derivations from art history, from past masters, but there is always a lightness to these borrowings. The past is not a burden nor a debt to be repaid. Finally, there is never a wasted brushstroke or an unclear area, every splotch of color and soak of oil is there for a reason. To sum up, there are winningly numerous ways in which the paintings can be viewed and understood.

— Joe Fyfe

The majority of the canvases are portraits and fêtes galantes, whose subjects possess the appropriately worshipful and hopeless gaze of Watteau's dancers, his commedia dell'arte stock characters, his courtly lovers enveloped in the haziest sfumato, and that other fêtes galantes look (altogether more carnal and deliberately, inappropriately, knowing), with scenes and scenarios calling to mind Marcantonio Raimondi's erotic illustrations for Pietro Aretino to the Marquis de Sade's less radical, more "workably" porno confrères, such as Restif de la Bretonne. All dirty pictures, all agreeably social.

These preponderantly French-y references are very much pointed: the artist's greater program both in "formal gestures" and iconography is redolently, resolutely Francophile: Matisse reigns supreme in Dougherty's referential aerie, along with Bonnard's decaying nudes in the bathtub, Marie Laurencin's most intimate friends and, across the Atlantic, Walt Kuhn's circus people and Alex Katz's urbane milieu. The artist's perverse figuration is decidedly Gustonesque, but it's articulated with a frillier version of his Grand Guignol.

Excerpt from Borrowed Time at Cheim and Read review
—David Rimanelli (Artforum, 2023)

"Some people can sing, some can't. It's the same with painting.

Maureen Dougherty knows color (beautiful color) and surface and light and space.

For years I would run into this very intent and independent figure at a museum or a gallery and wonder who she was.

She was one of the very few people actually looking at the paintings. A sweet smile here and there and then she was off.

Eventually, she invited me to a few very surprising and impressive studio visits and we put together a show.

I learned that for Maureen, there really is no difference between figuration and abstraction—they are interchangeable and coexist.

Her painting has life, humour, and an effortlessness that reminds me of Matisse, Katz and Walt Kuhn."

— John Cheim

AG: Given your technical virtuosity and facility with paint handling, it's hard to believe you haven't been painting figurative works your whole career! Can you speak about your journey from abstraction to figuration? How did it happen?

MD: My work required traveling outside of my New York City studio. I went around the world, bringing back the light and content to my work. I had been roaming Greece not long before the pandemic and came back with an image of the head of Athena and a tiny owl sculpture I'd spent most of the trip searching for. I found it in a box of junk at an Athens flea market. In some ways, I can attribute that trip to my return to the formal figure. I became obsessed with painting Athena and her owl together and separately. My last trip before moving out of the city studio was to Morocco, which was devoid of women, just color texture, and repeated symmetrical tiles.

What is important to mention about the relationship between the two genres is that the scale of my figurative work is boundless, most likely due to my "two fucks to the wind" abstract painting approach. In any form of art, I work until I achieve a convincing presence or, as I like to say, "an angle of repose" in a painting. The momentum of my process is like that of a stone rolling down the face of a mountain, being carried along until it suddenly stops and plants itself in its final position.

There is a "letting go" process which involves muscle memory of pleasure. It's believing and not believing in oneself during the course of a painting. The process always wins but loses when there are no more mountains to climb. My process is always to be reaching.

If I choose to return to abstraction, so be it. Though I am at a place I have always wanted to be, at a very young age, I declared I wanted to paint like Raphael which left me off balance. To this day, he still does; his sensuality was and still is the trigger for me. Like a stick of TNT, his surface threatens to burst. I was attracted to that then and now. Images should always be threatening to ask questions and confront the viewer. It's such a great idea to chase such beauty—I'll continue. I adore art, particularly great, big, fearless, magnificent, elevating paintings. Ecstasy is a drug for me; it's standing in front of a great painting.

AG: Women are a topical and eternal subject! Why are "women" a compelling vehicle for your painting practice? This also begs the question about your methods in terms of subject matter. Are you working from found images? Imagination? A combo?

MD: Regarding returning to the figure, I started painting figuratively in this small room given to me in a house outside of New York City during the pandemic. Out the window, a white car was parked and never moved. I had never drawn a car before. I got into its symmetry, particularly the rearview mirrors and tinted glass windows swooping down the back to the trunk. I didn't realize how sexy and figurative cars were. This was when I re-entered my love of symmetrical form and the figure.

Living in isolation like everyone else, I constantly streamed the internet. I followed a trans-rapper named Young Ma primarily because of the comments that ensued from his/her posts. Who were these bodies of young girls and boys—shaking their asses in the shallow of a pool? For what or whom were they doing it—Young Ma or moi?

That intrigued me. I approached the content confrontationally in my work because I didn't know it existed until a young editor told me about the phenomenon of "Only Fans" and the income stream it generates. I have never opened an Only Fans account but have followed that internet rabbit hole into other dimensions. I liked it for its disgrace of purity and thought it was excellent subject matter, and it still is. My images are open to interpretation. They deal with human intimacy and connection. They are lacking in some detail, allowing the viewer to step in. The push and pull of innocence and maturity is deliberately blurred and rendered child-like as commentary on media and contemporary culture. If a cultural pretext is rarely explored in fine art, I'm about it in my painting.

I use photography occasionally, but I try to avoid it. I'm too impulsive to copy, and the studio has no internet, so I take a pulse from a photo or a position.

AG: Are you thinking about the male versus female gaze in how you construct your work? Or are you quoting the way American visual culture presumes feminine display for (primarily cis het male) consumption? As you are such an astute consumer of art history, you're also winking oftentimes at the gendered tropes and power structures that underlie the centuries of how women are represented in paint in the Western canon...

MD: I really don't have a preference for male or female; it's just that a lot of my males look female, and a lot of my females look male, so I really don't differentiate.

AG: Your women—even when they are tits out or posing in a performative way—retain agency, as well as painterly flair. Am I overreaching? Or is there a sly politics of sex positivity—or at least the power of self-exploitation coming off these fictional ladies?

MD: The painting itself must be muscular enough to hold place. So, in that regard, the female form is rendered whole, plastic, and impenetrable; it's really more abstract than it appears. Because I can't erase the historical content of paintings I've seen in the past 50 years, I'm constantly referring back to "the master" as a platform. The one difference in my work is the confrontational approach of the body. There's usually direct contact; there's nothing to the side or turned to the back; it's generally straight out, with no interference. The admission seems to say look at me! Here I am, in the flesh. Now what?

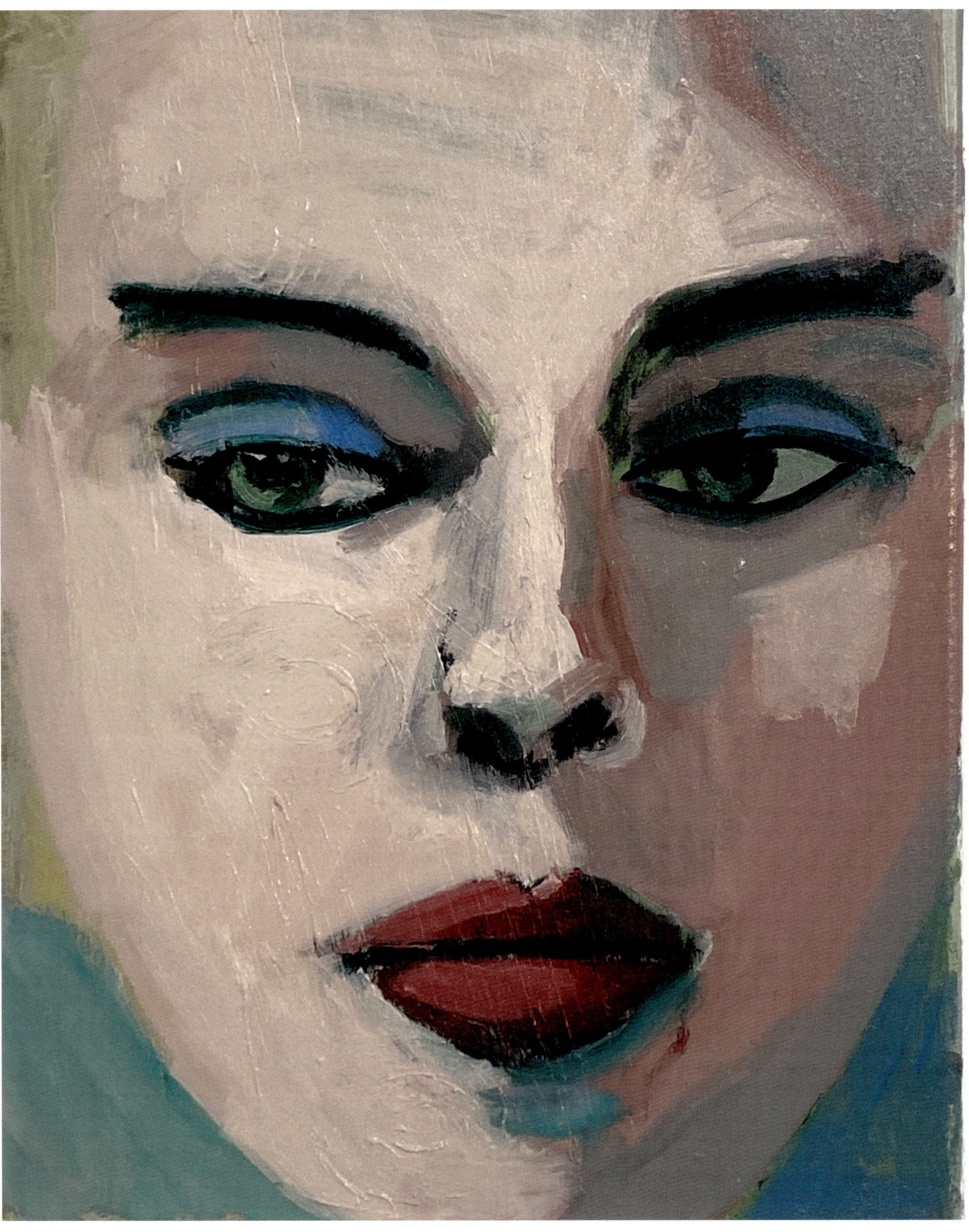

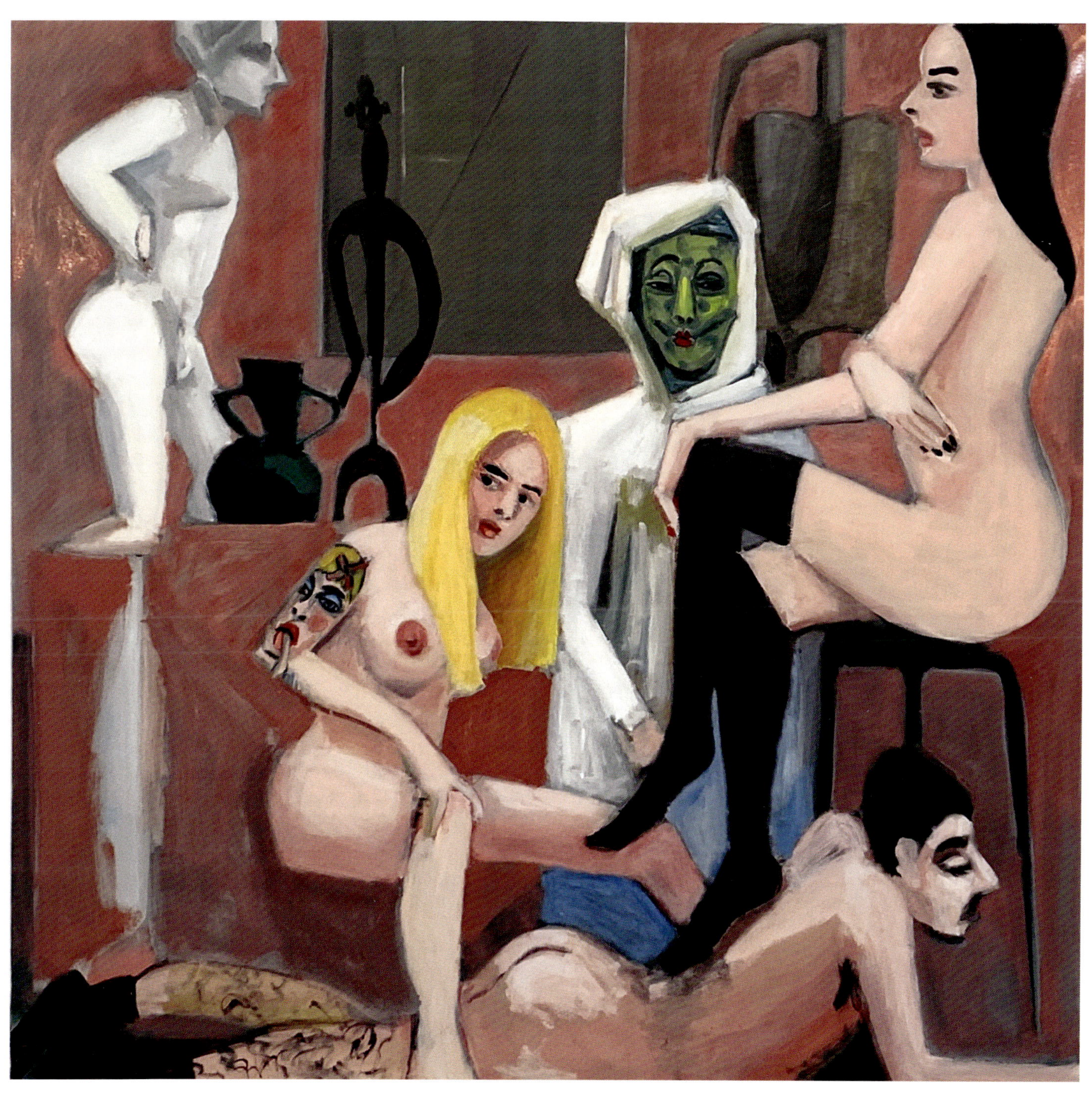

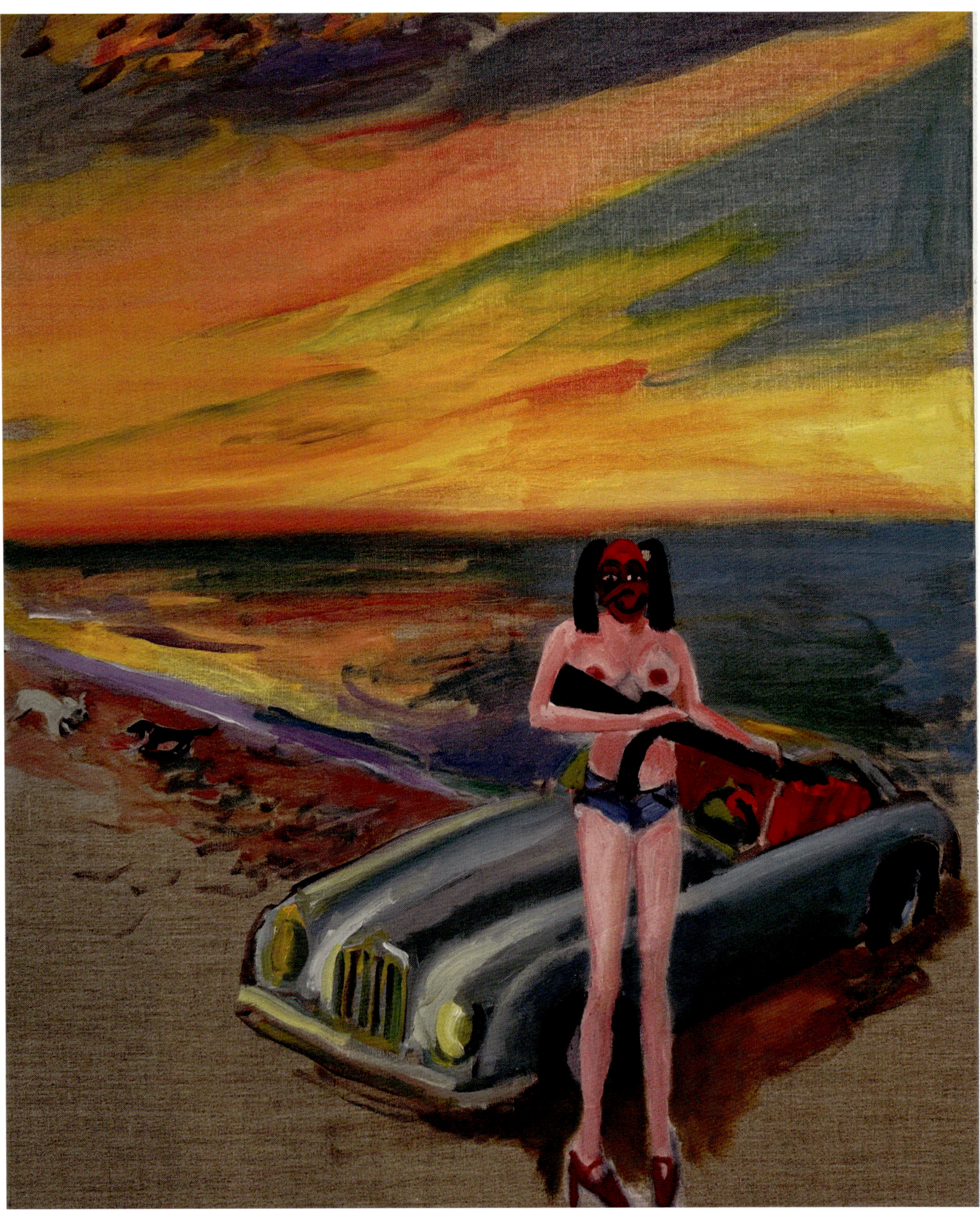

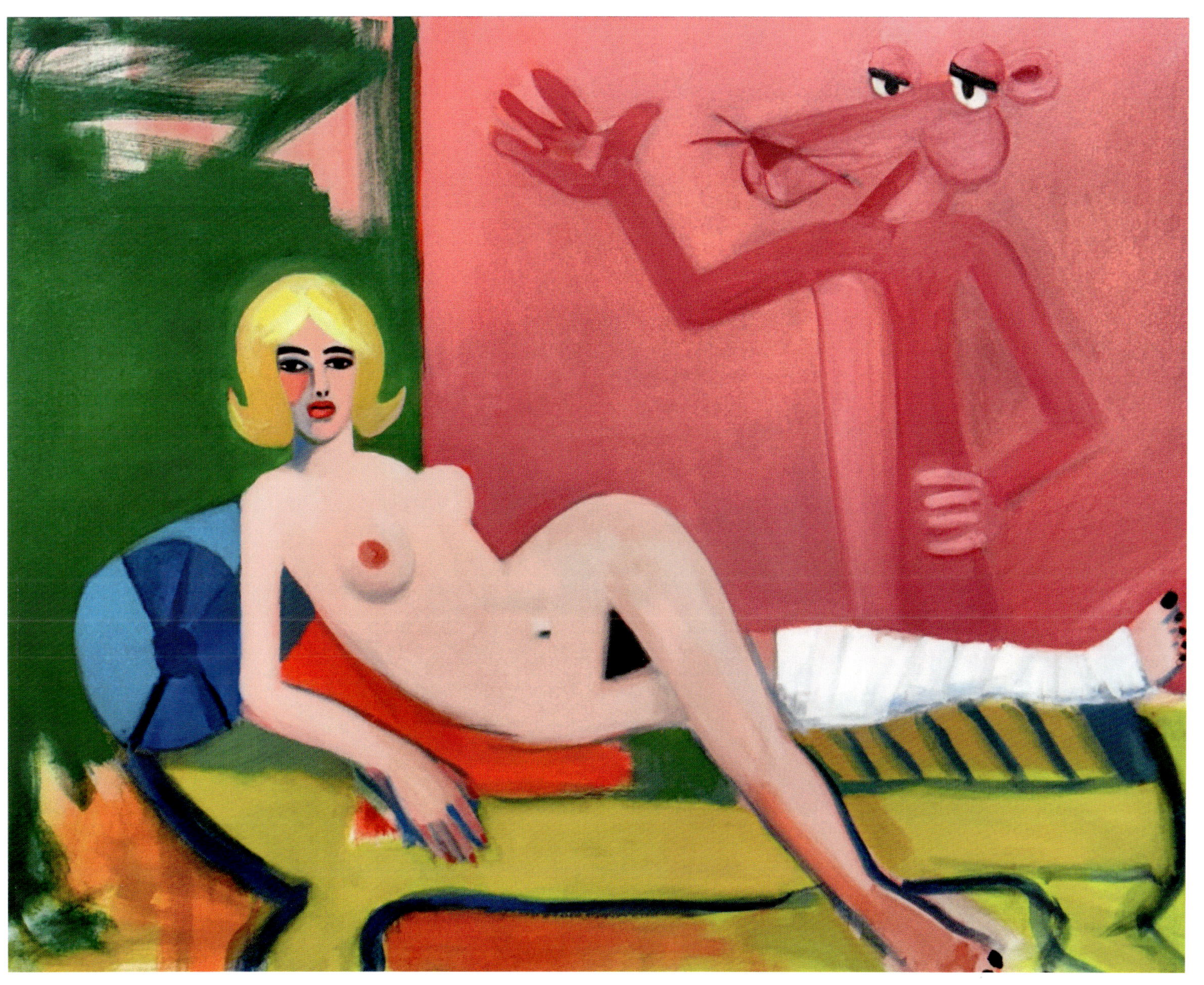

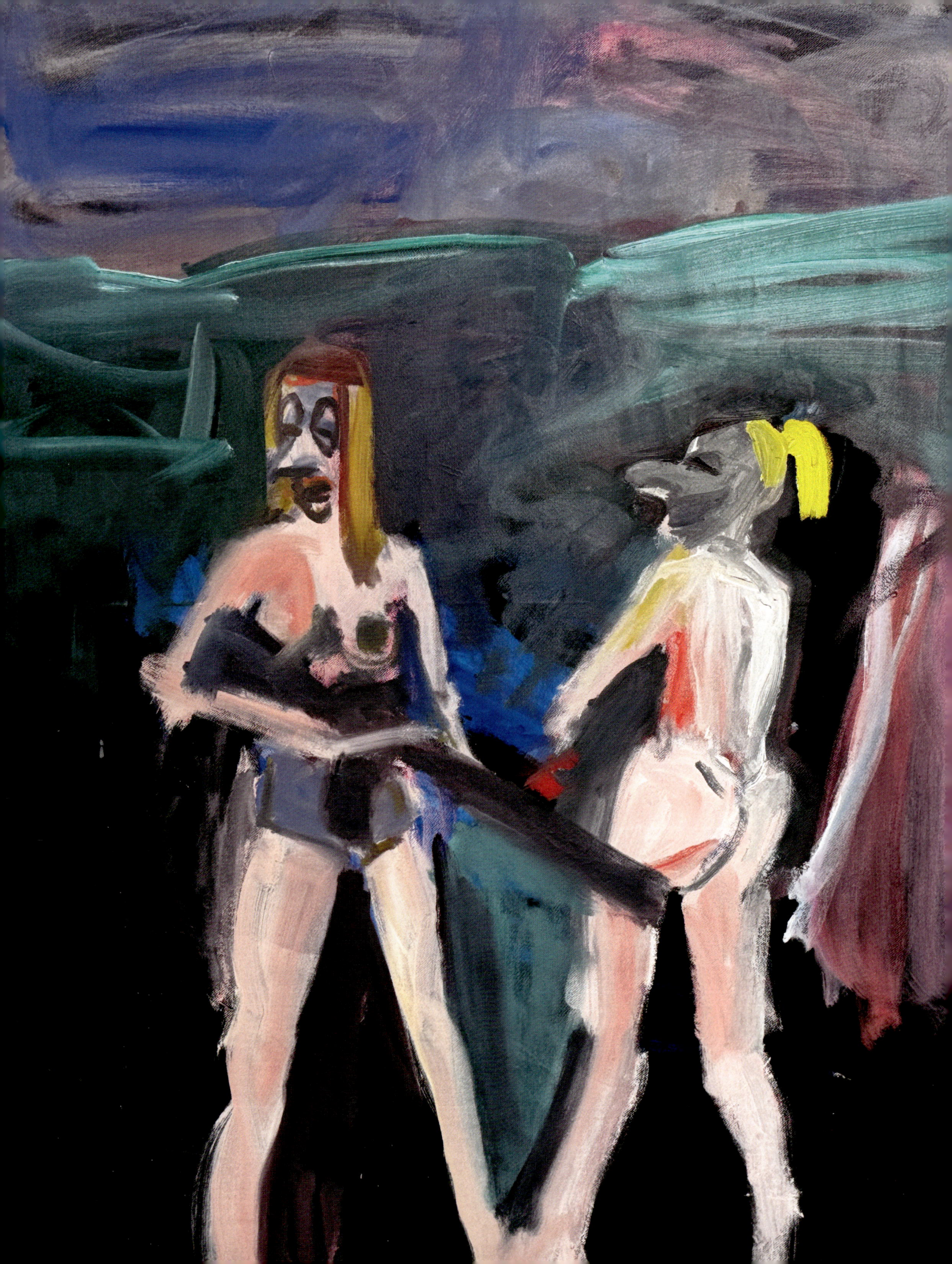

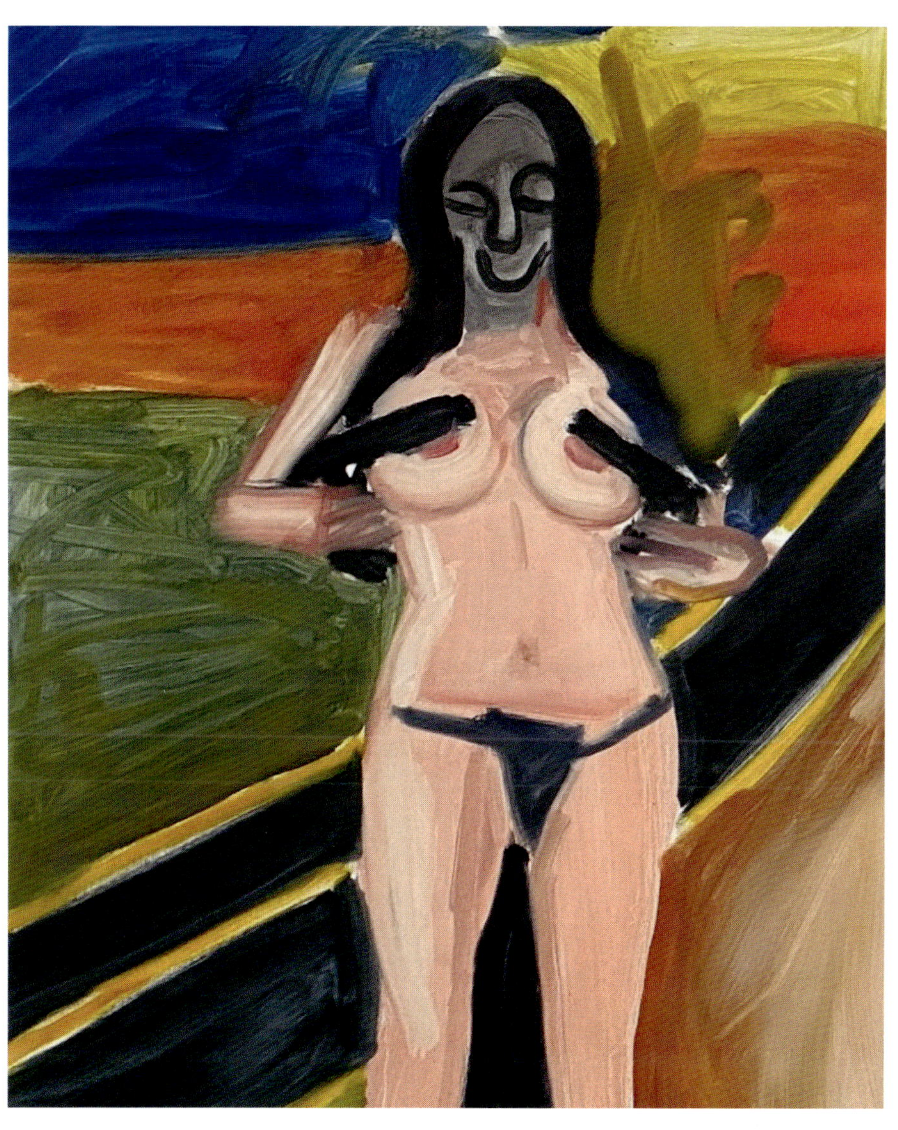

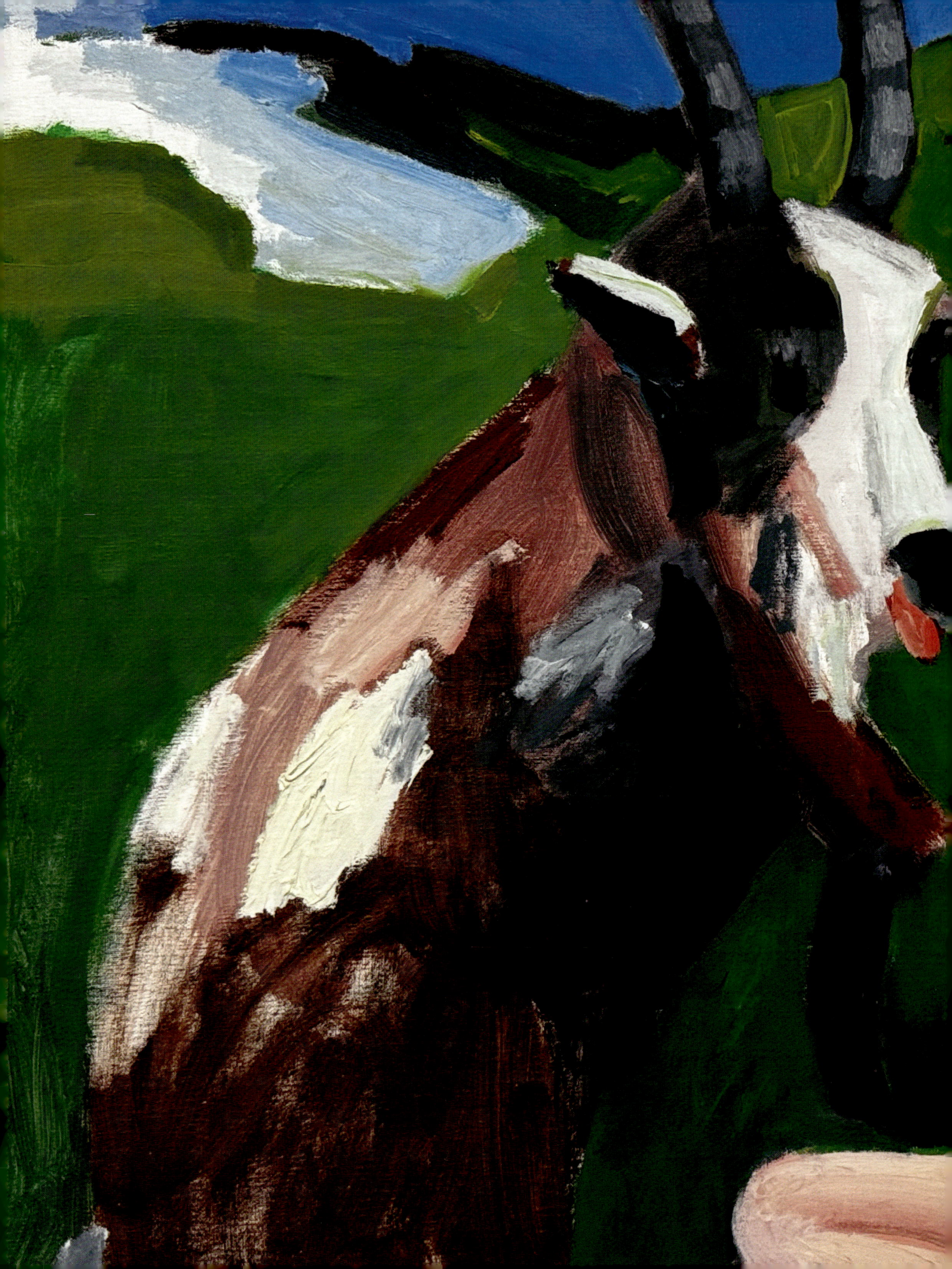

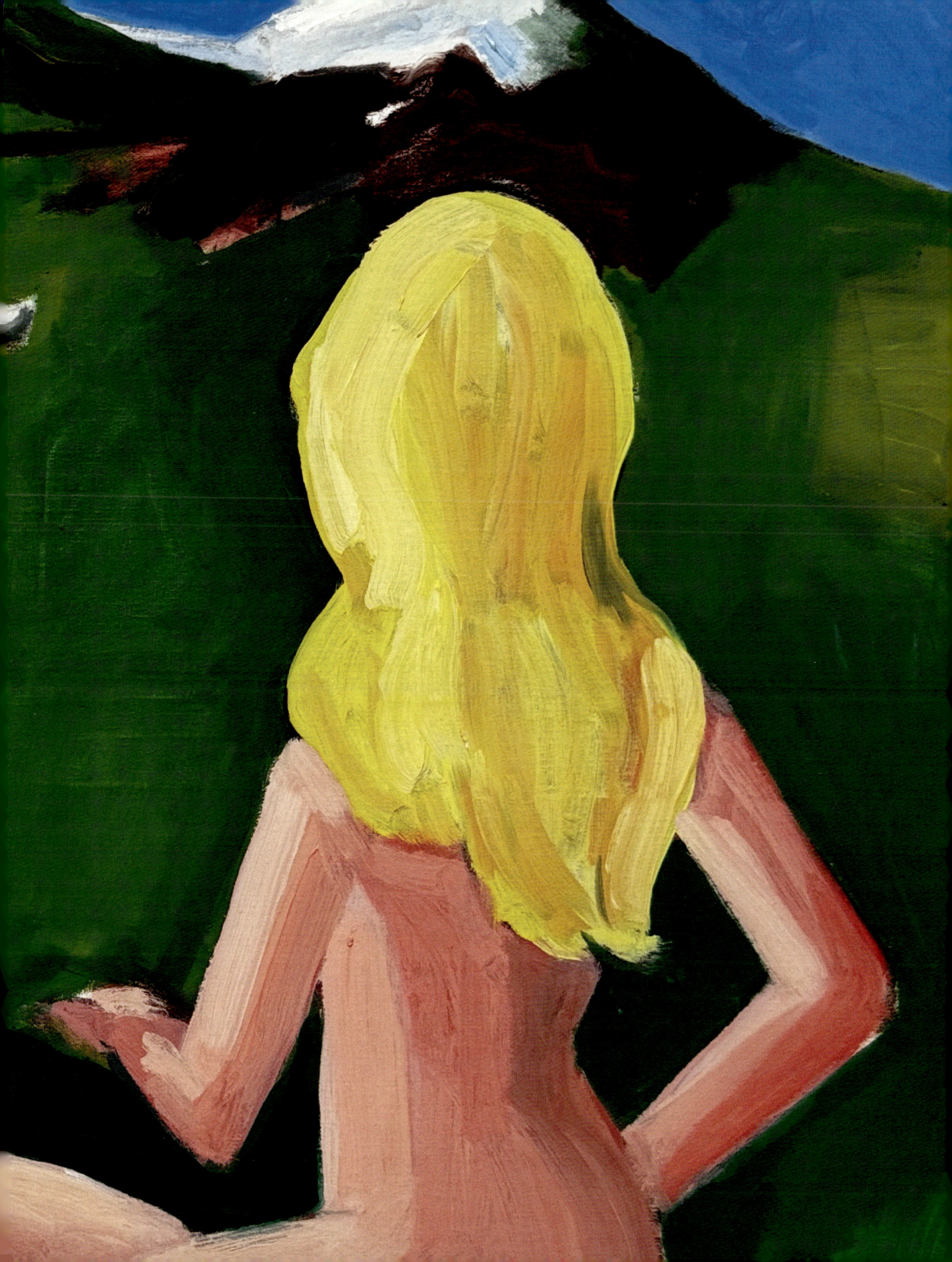

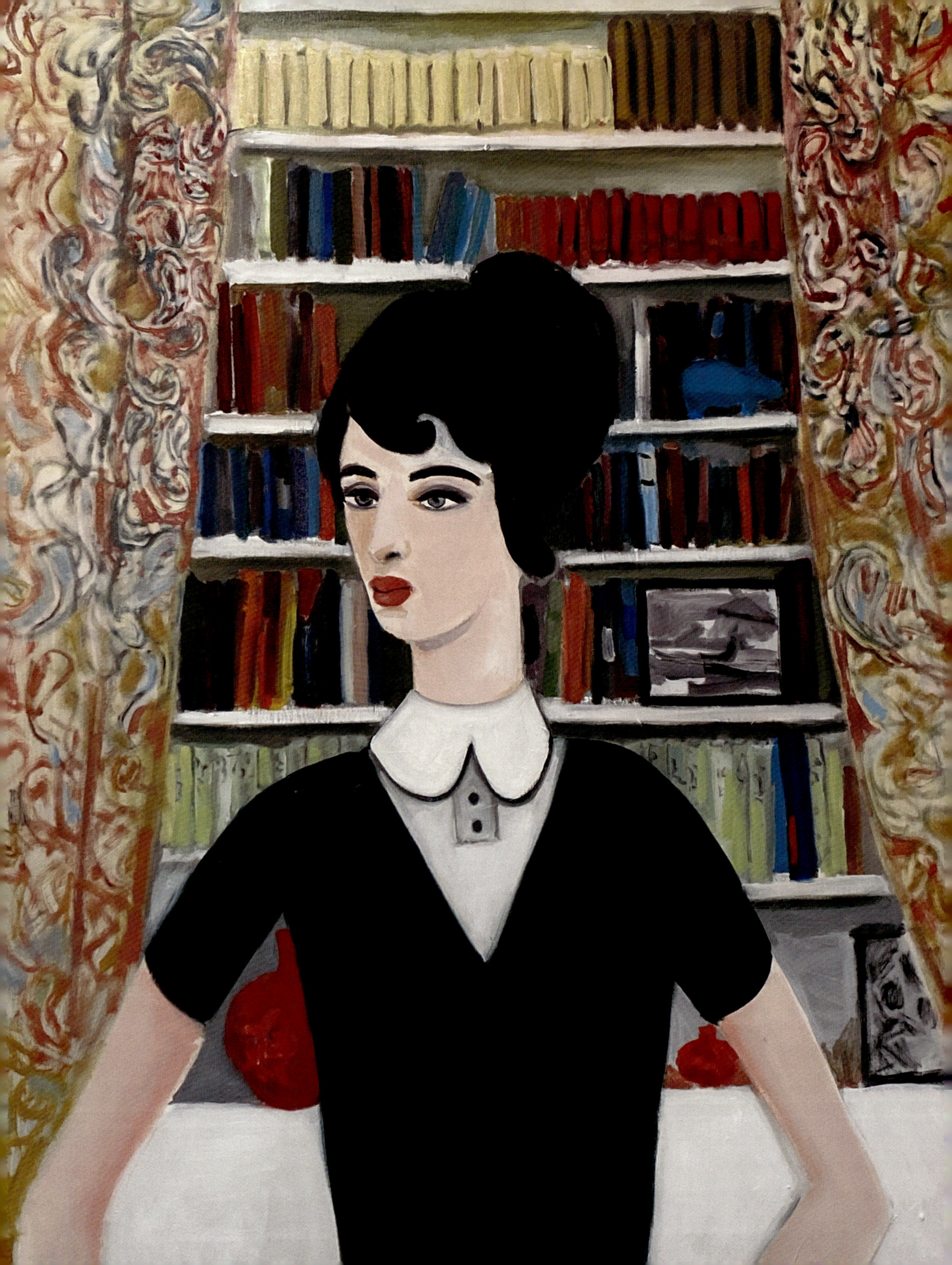

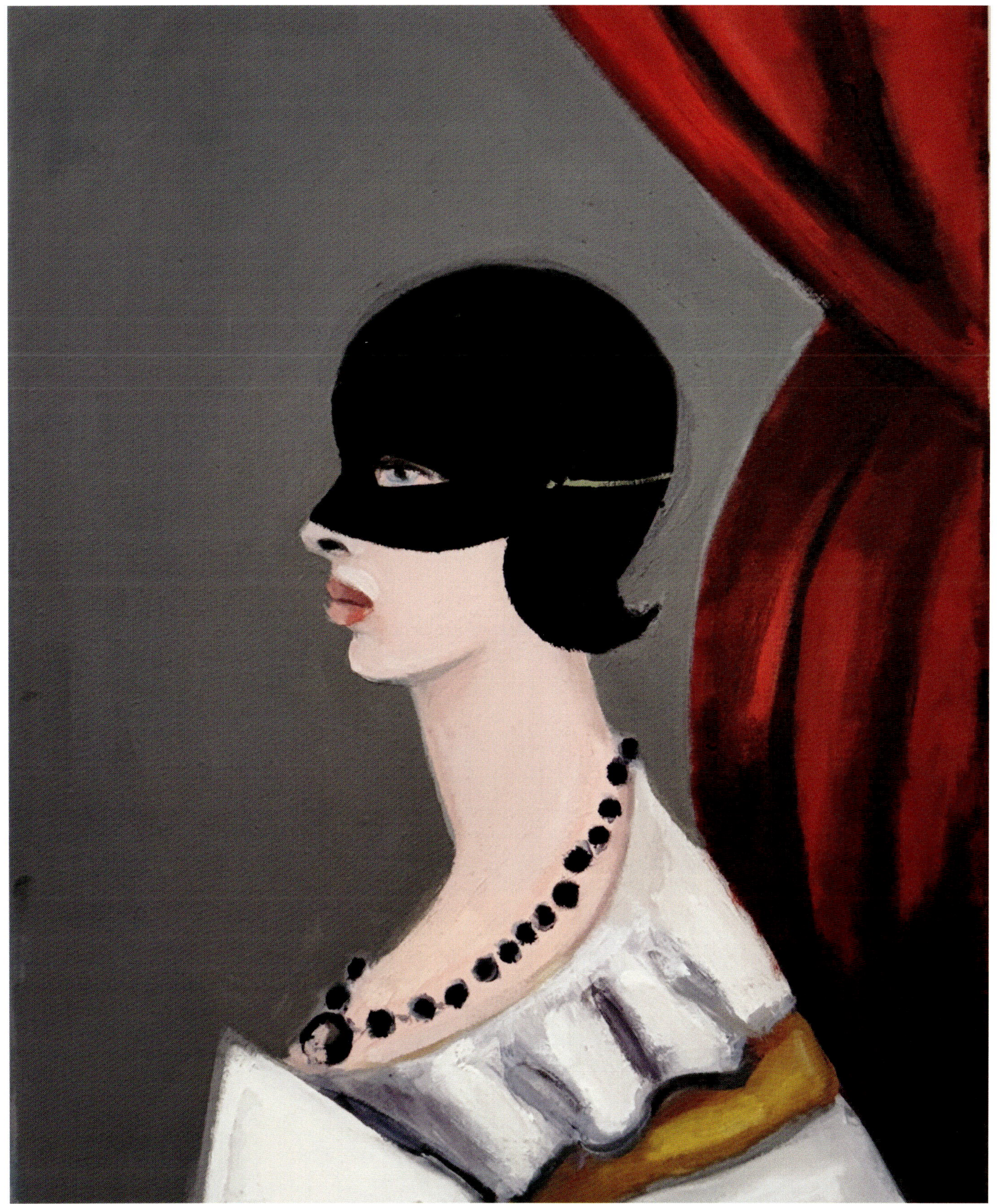

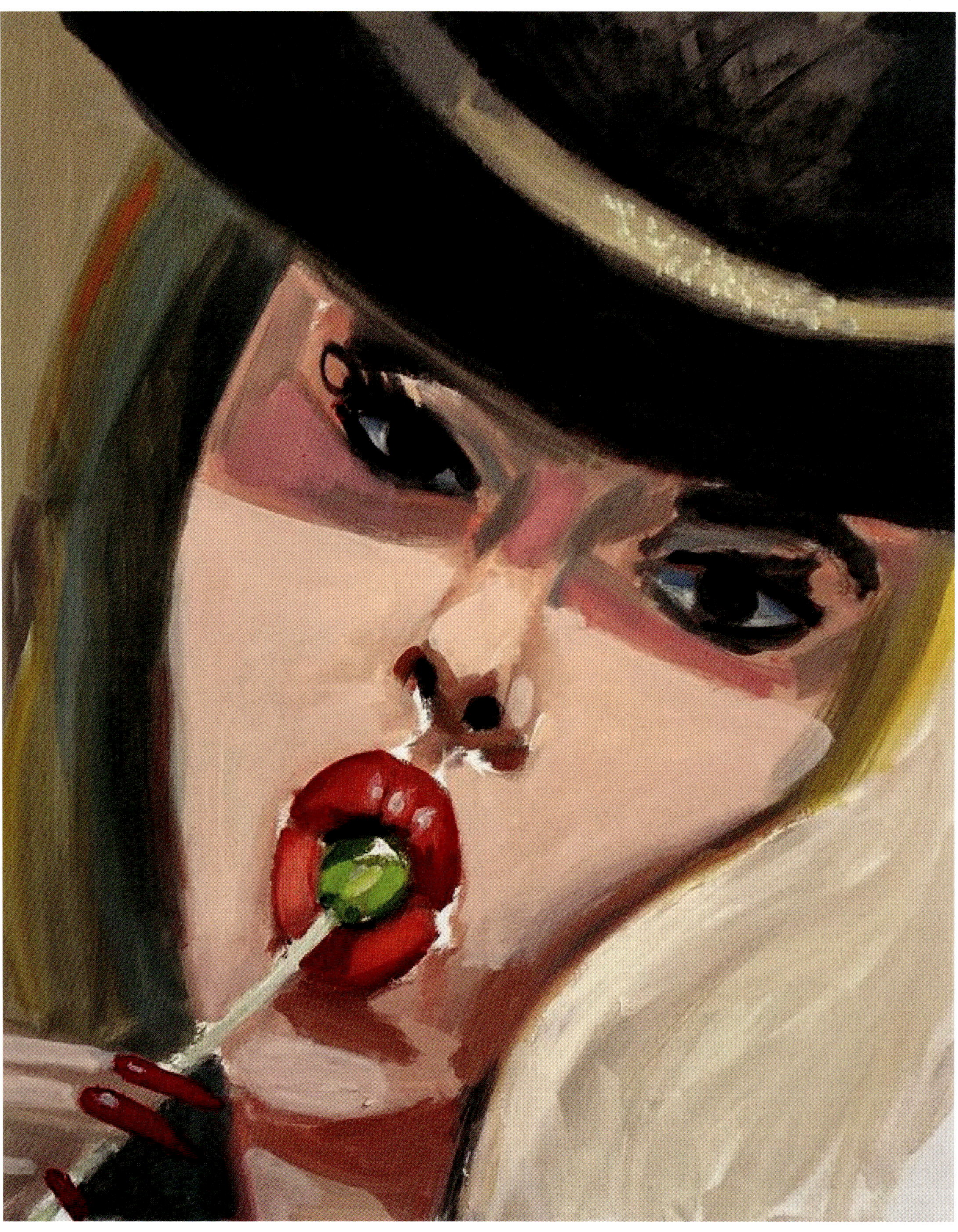

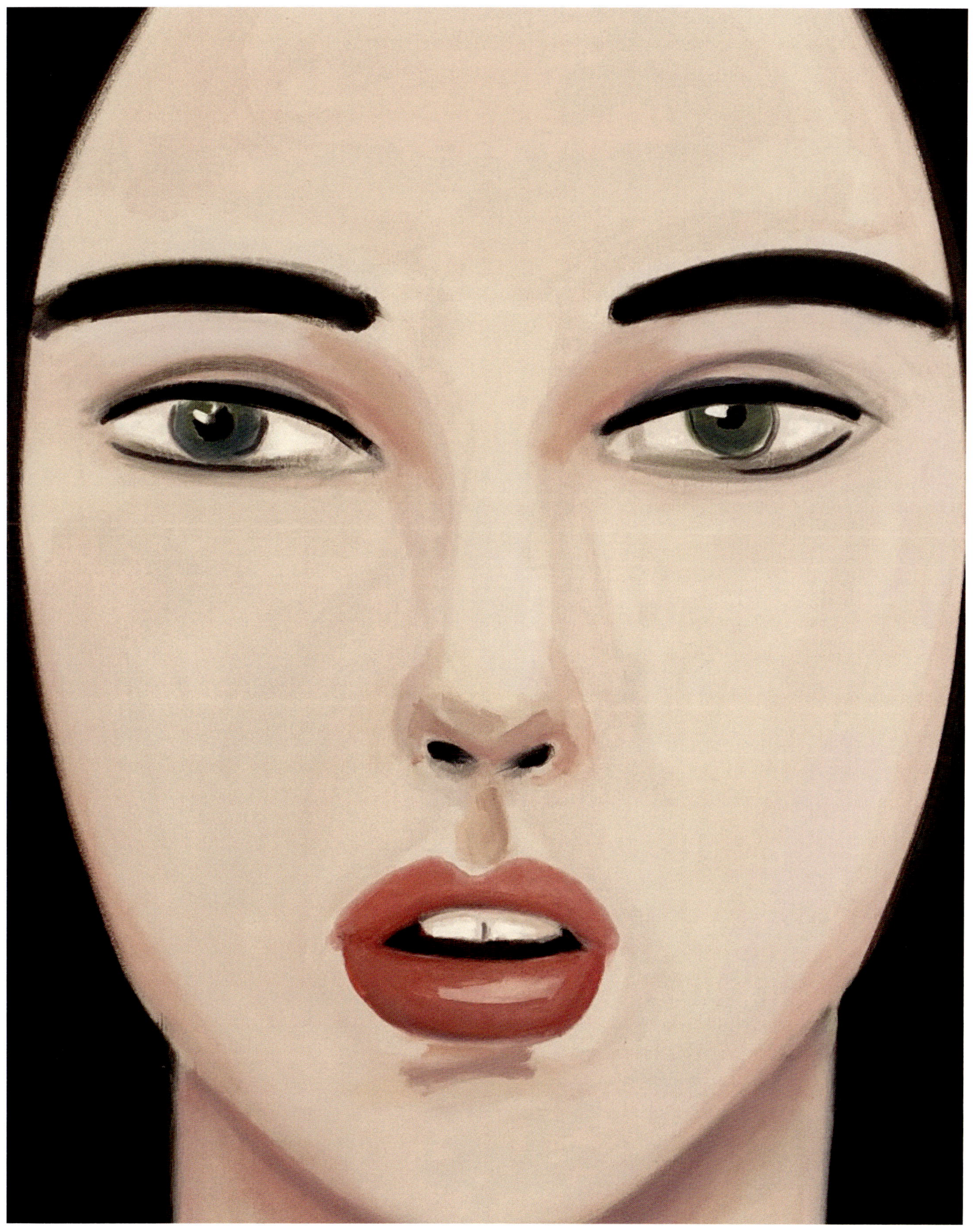

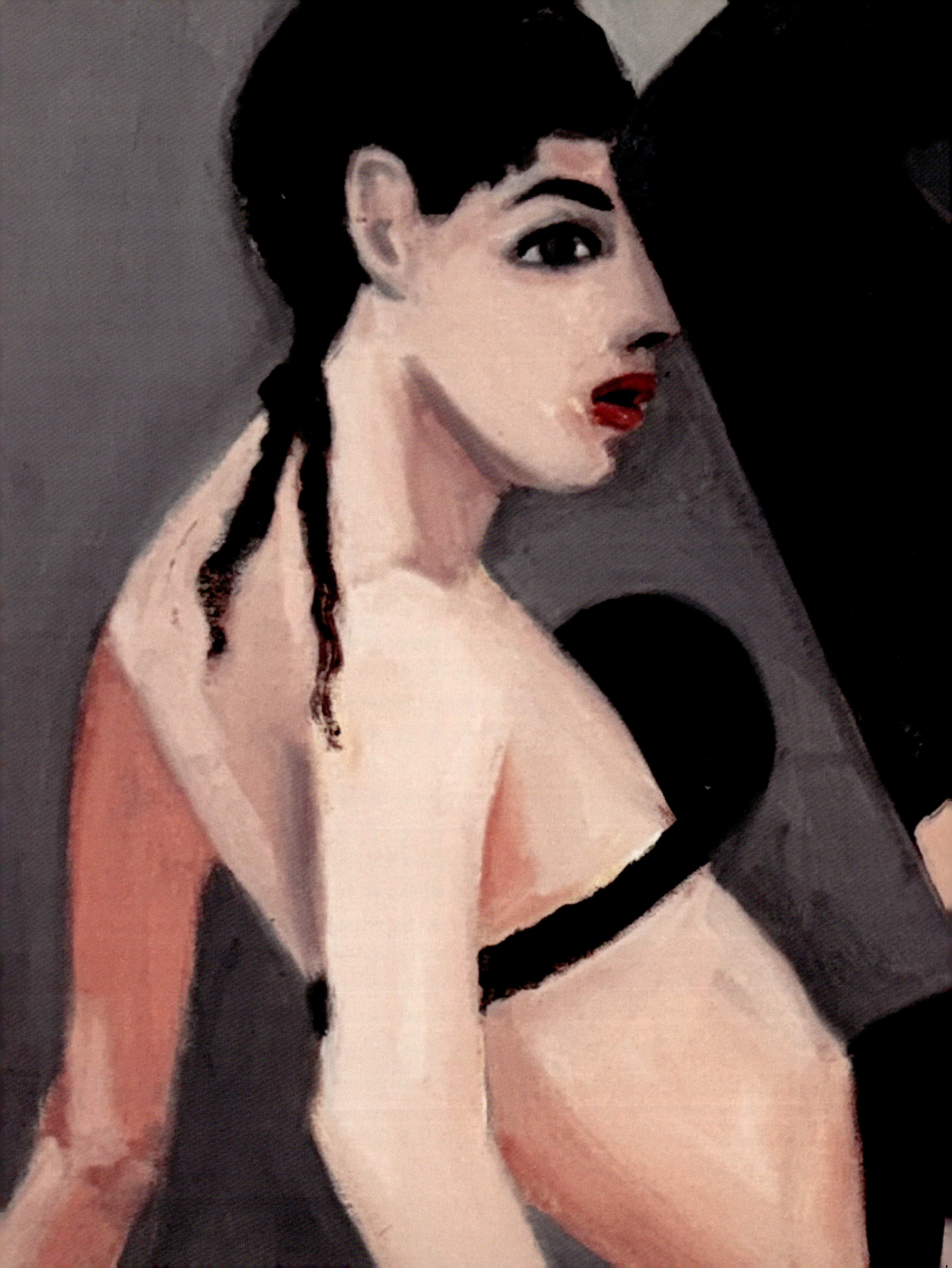

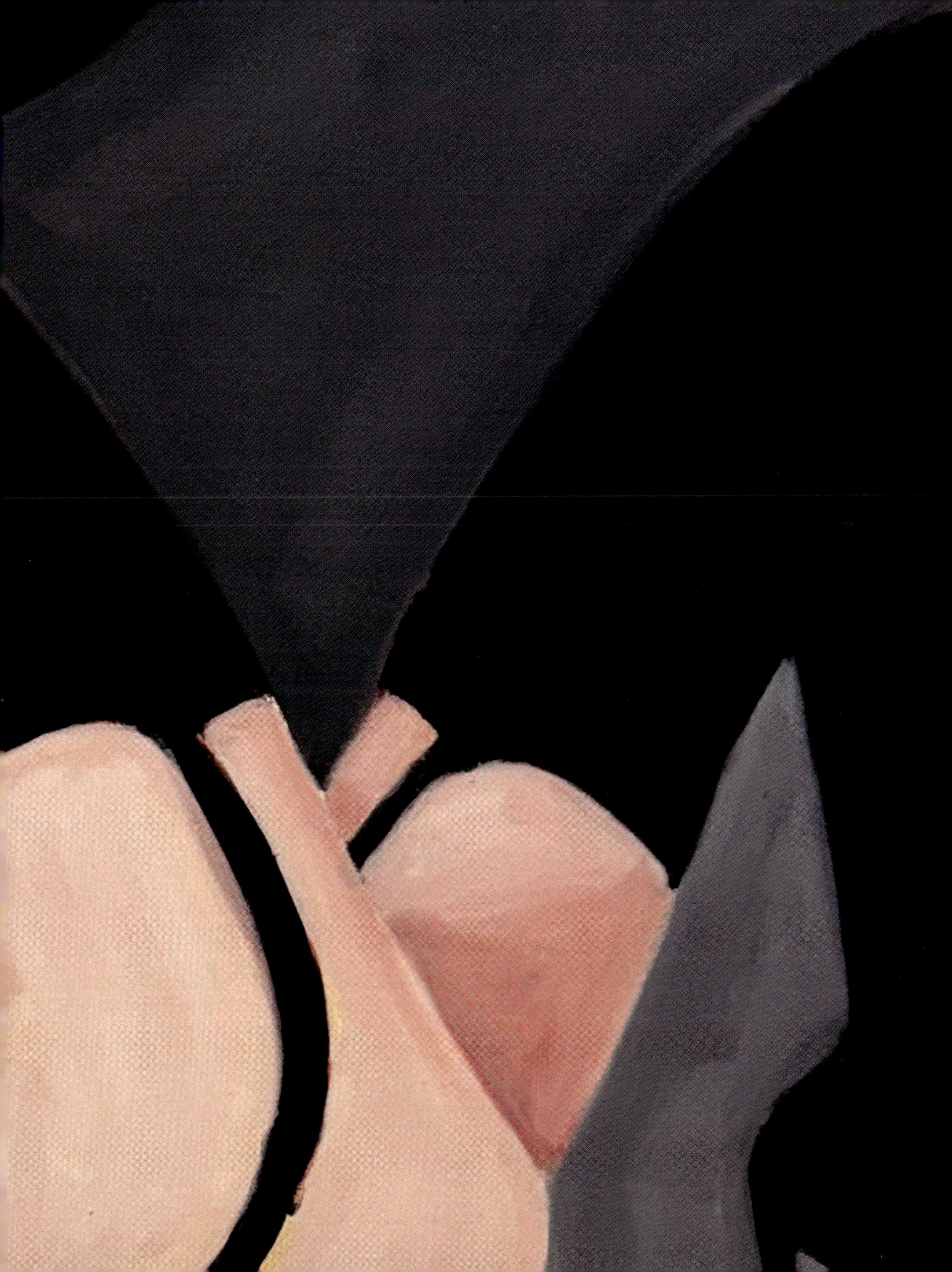

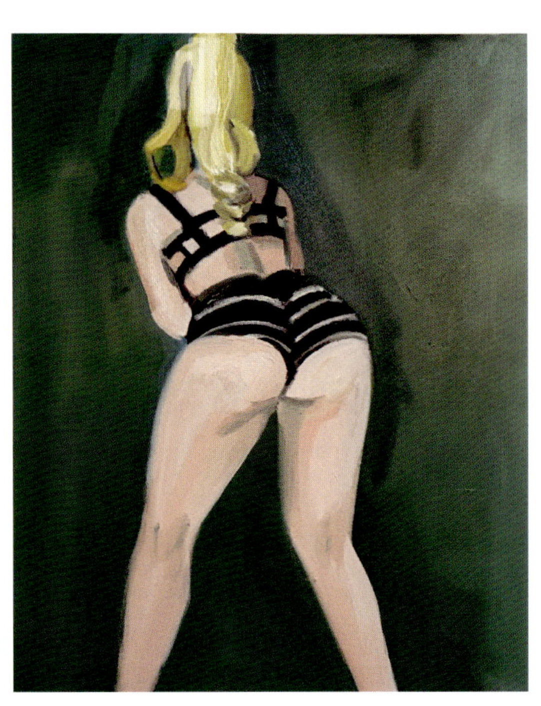

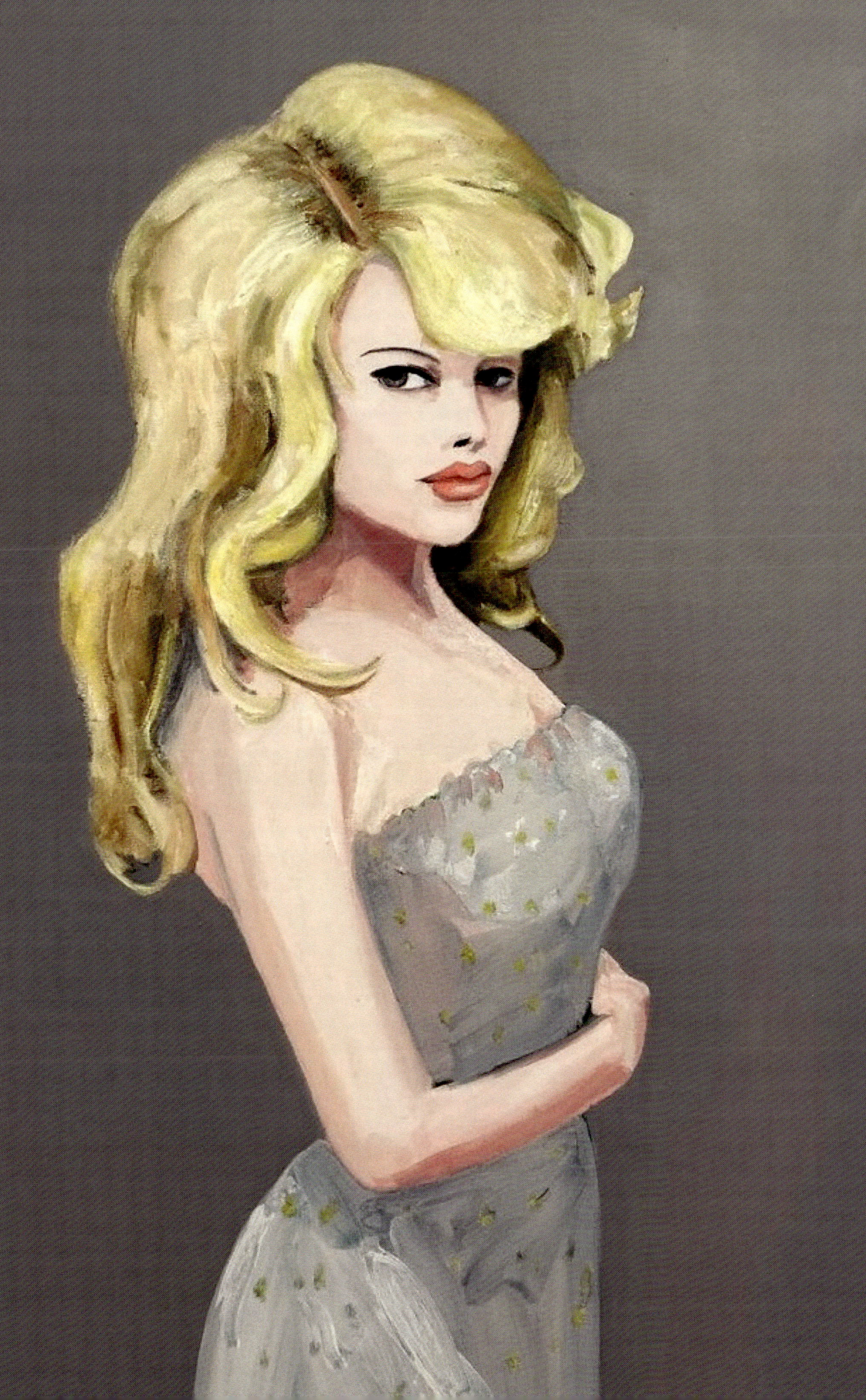

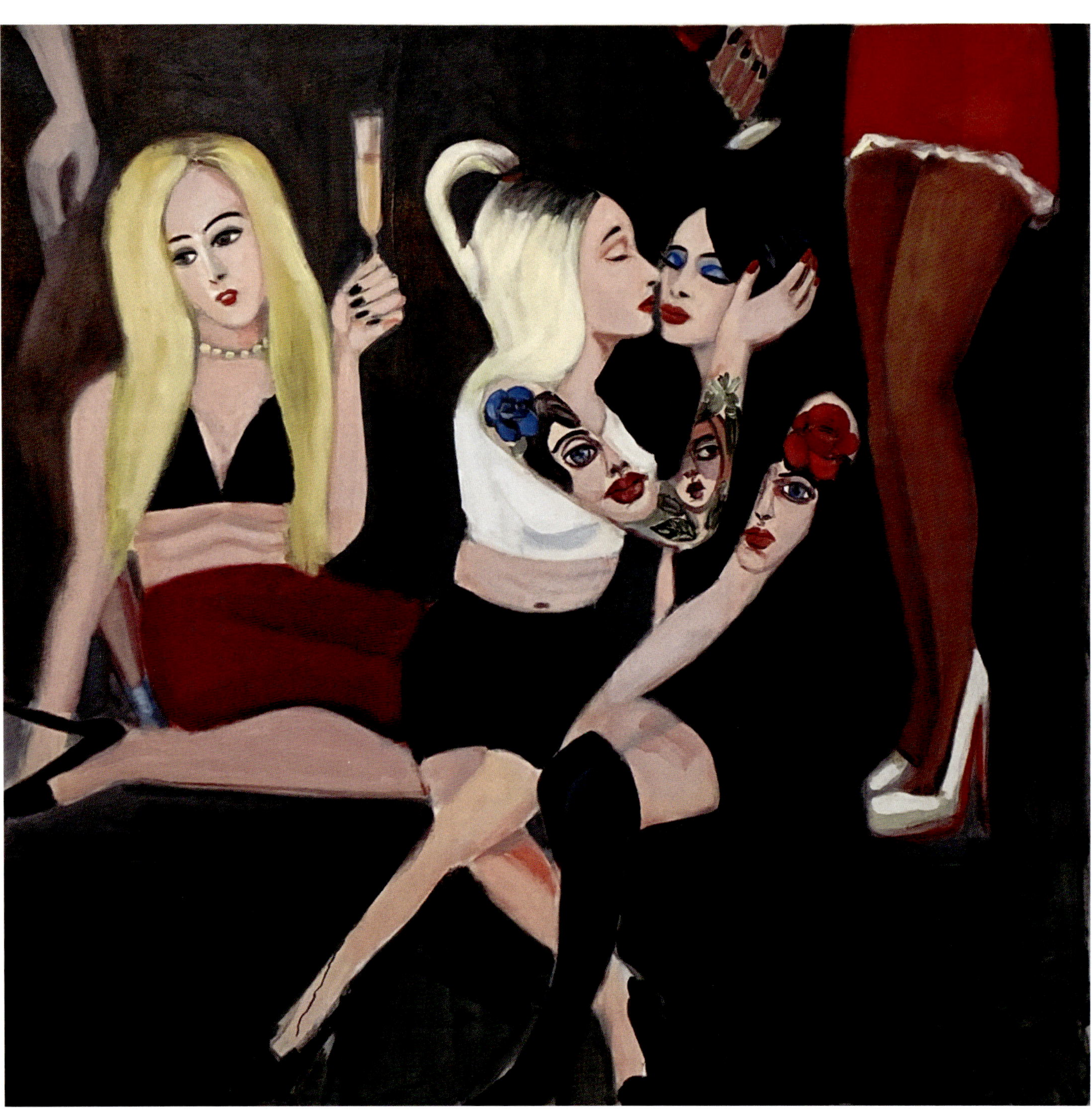

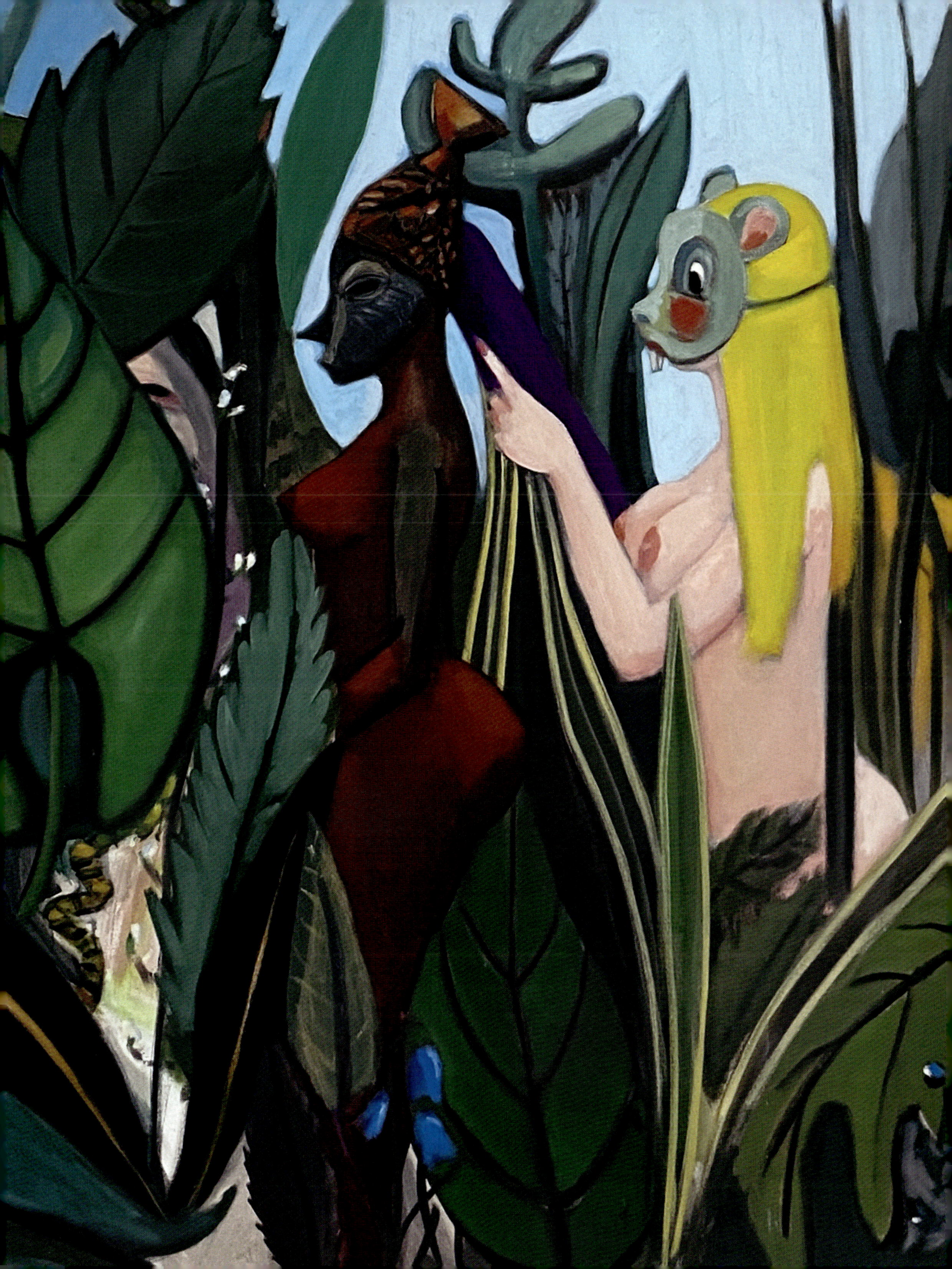

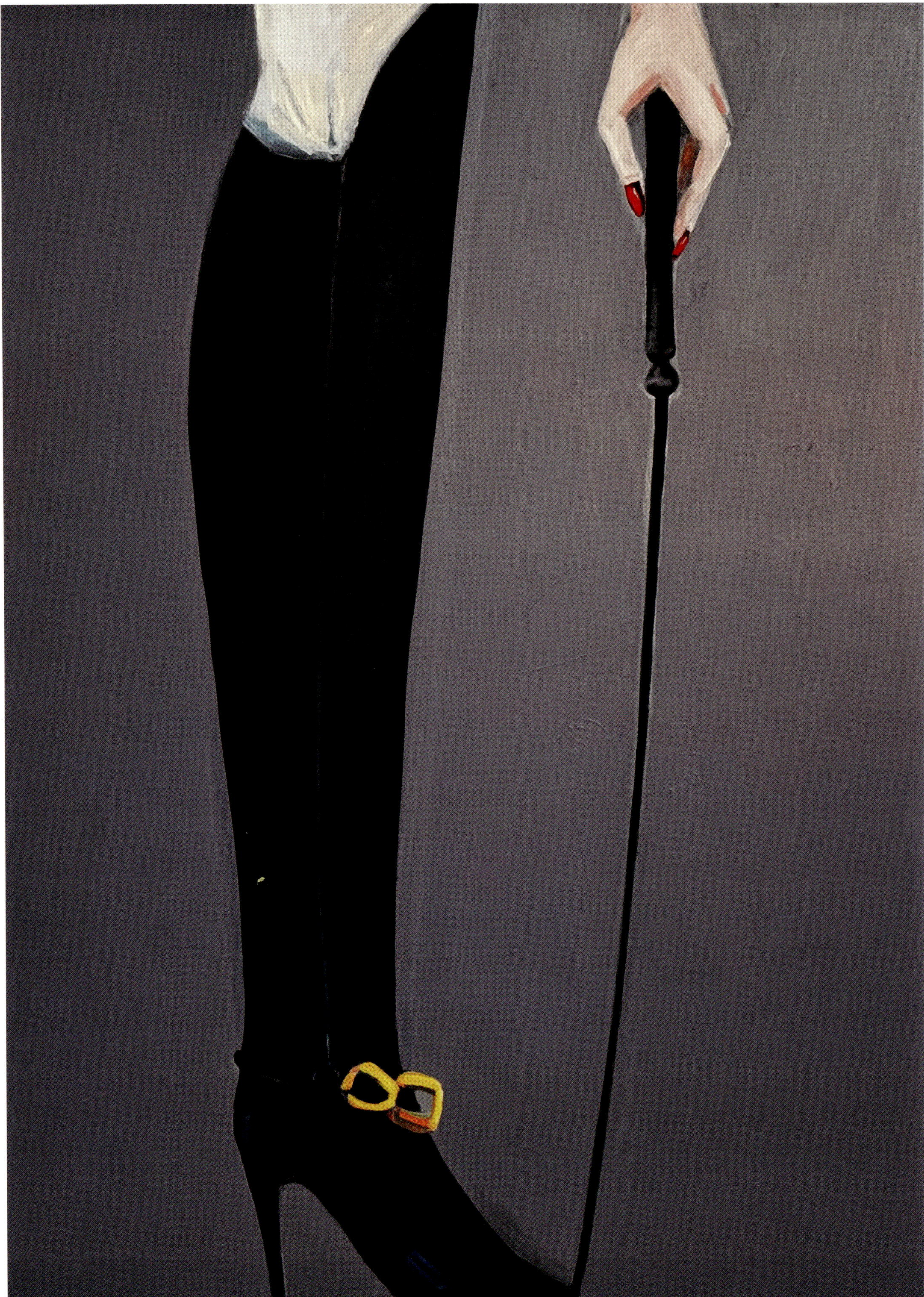

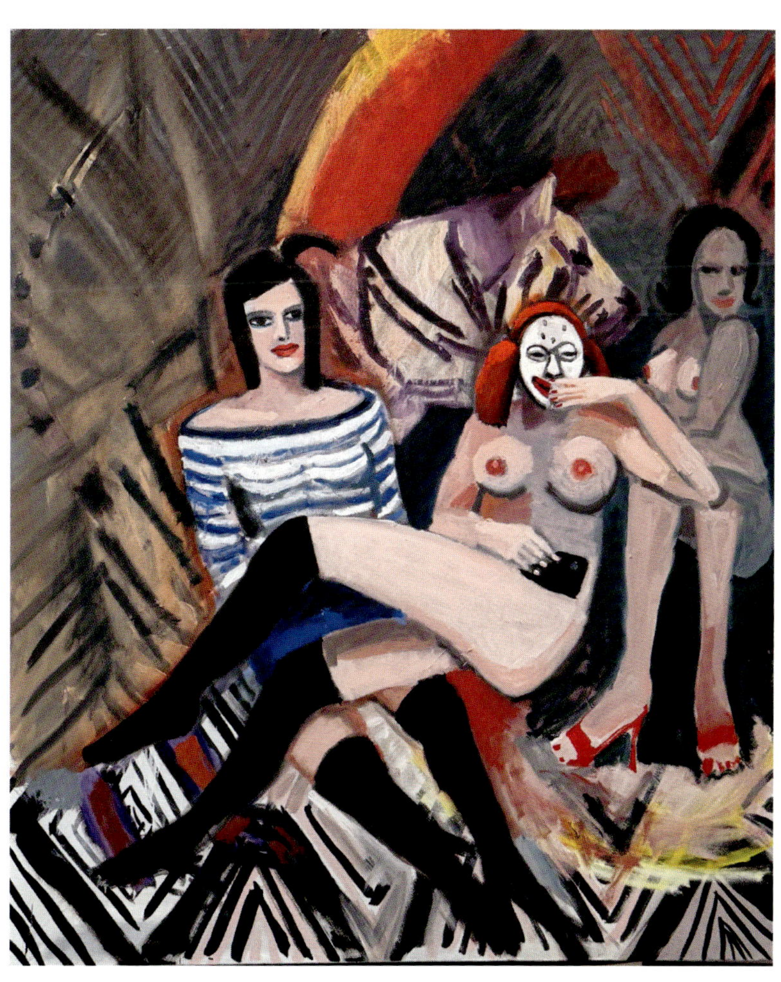

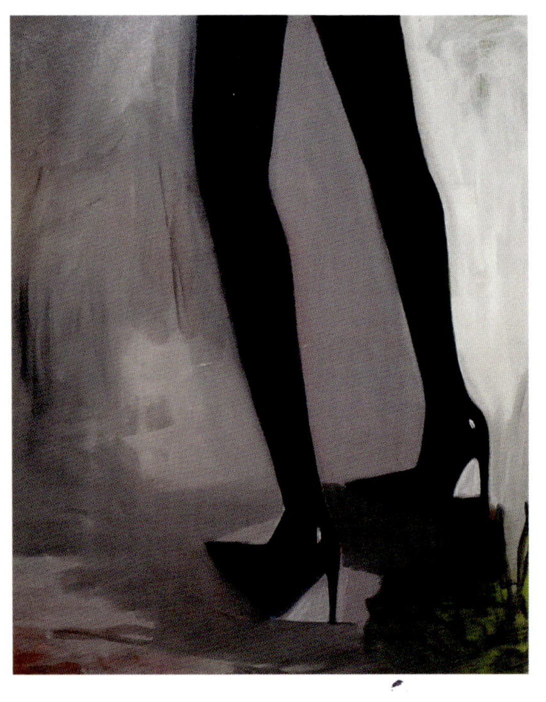

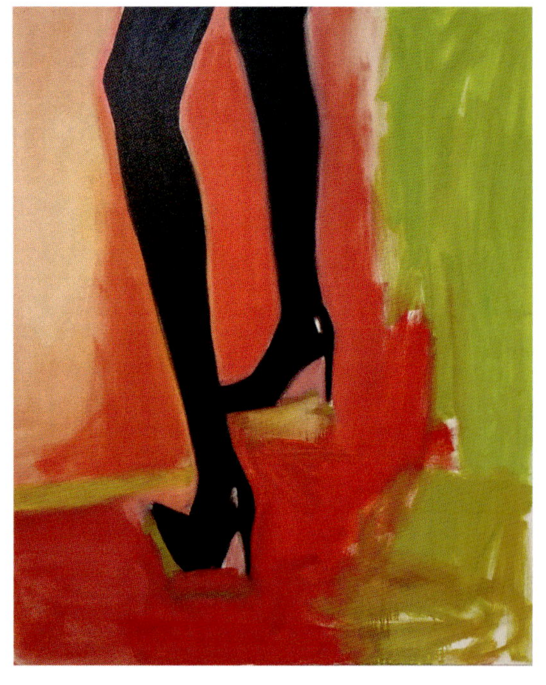

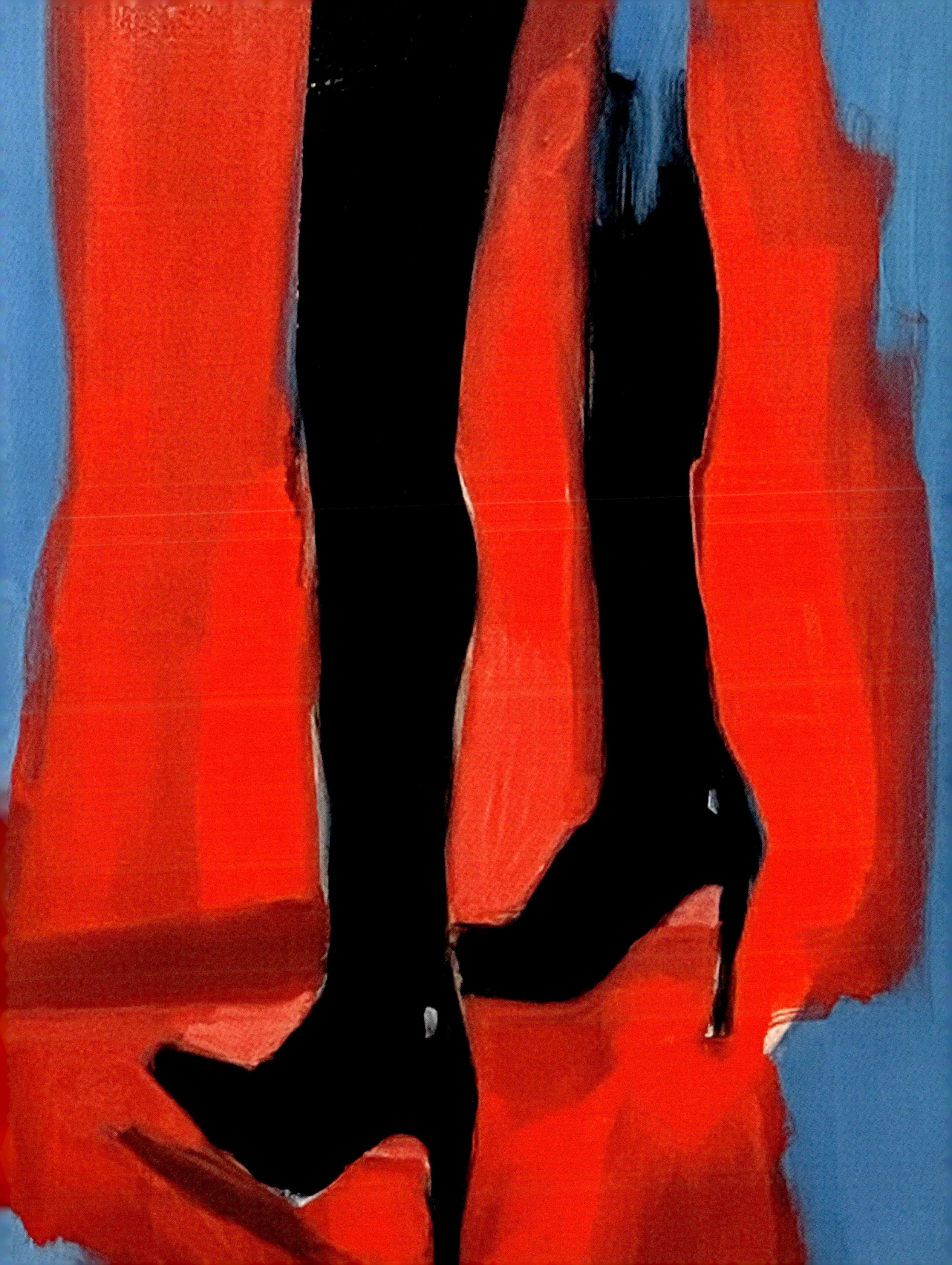

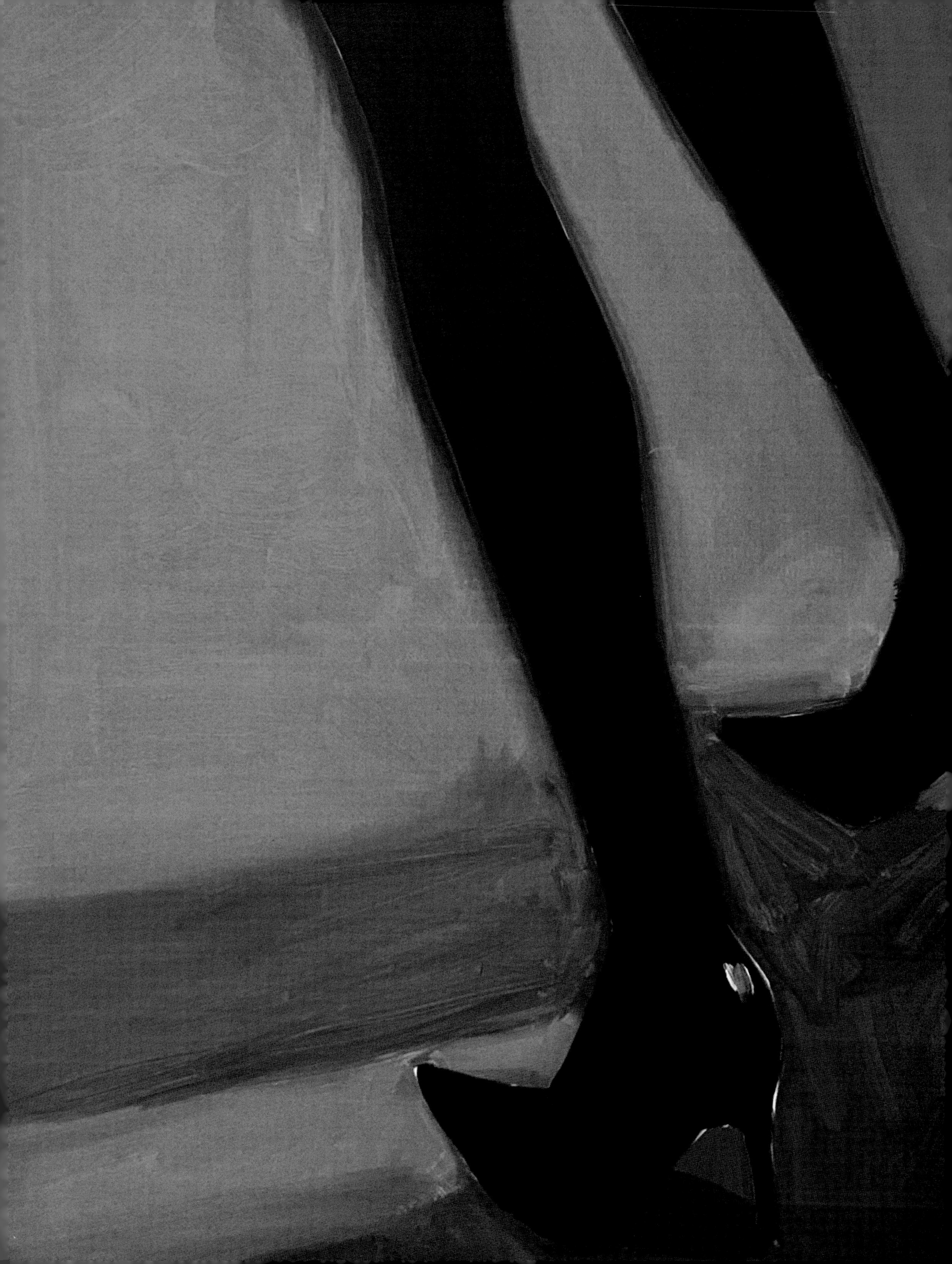

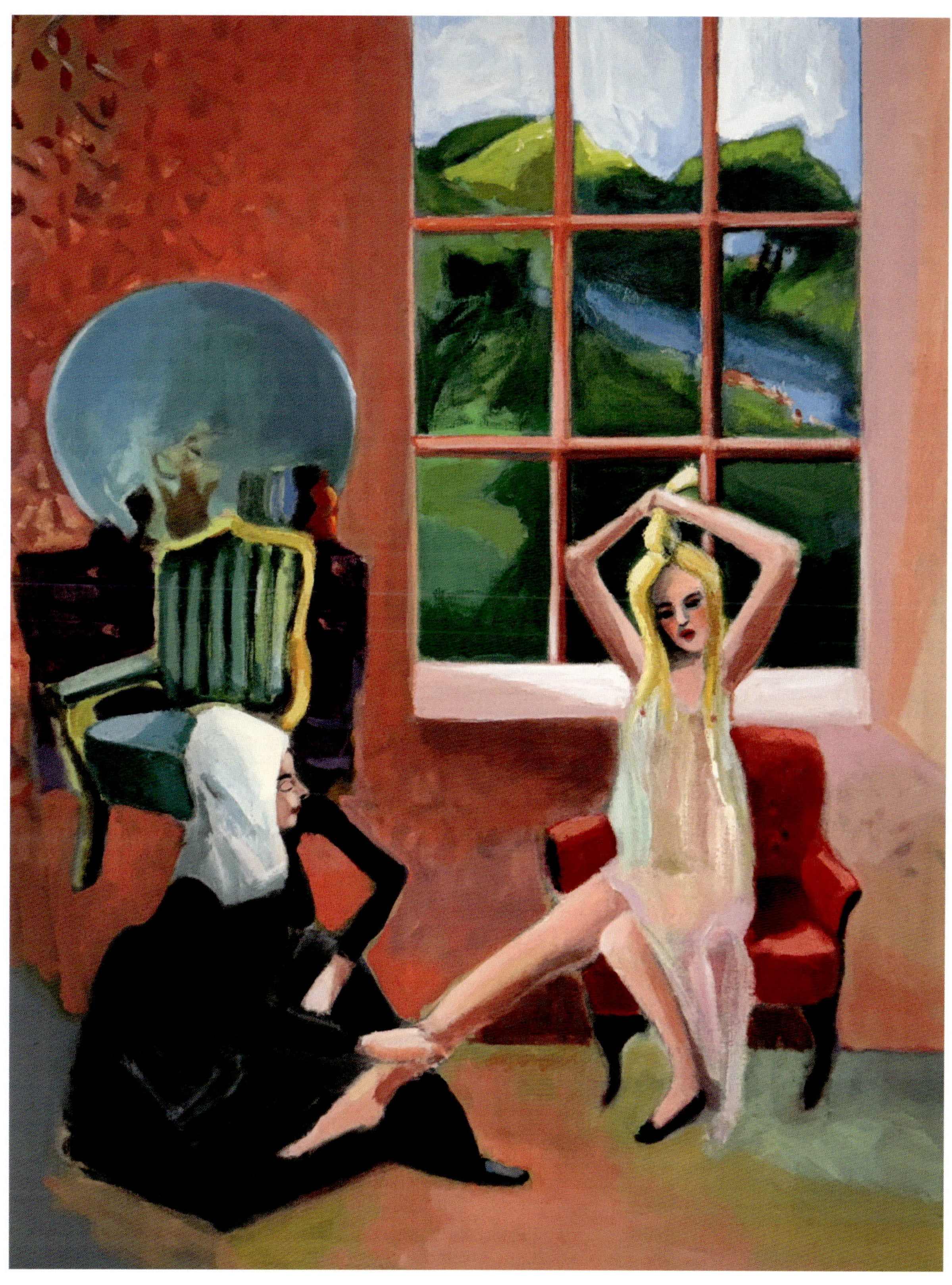

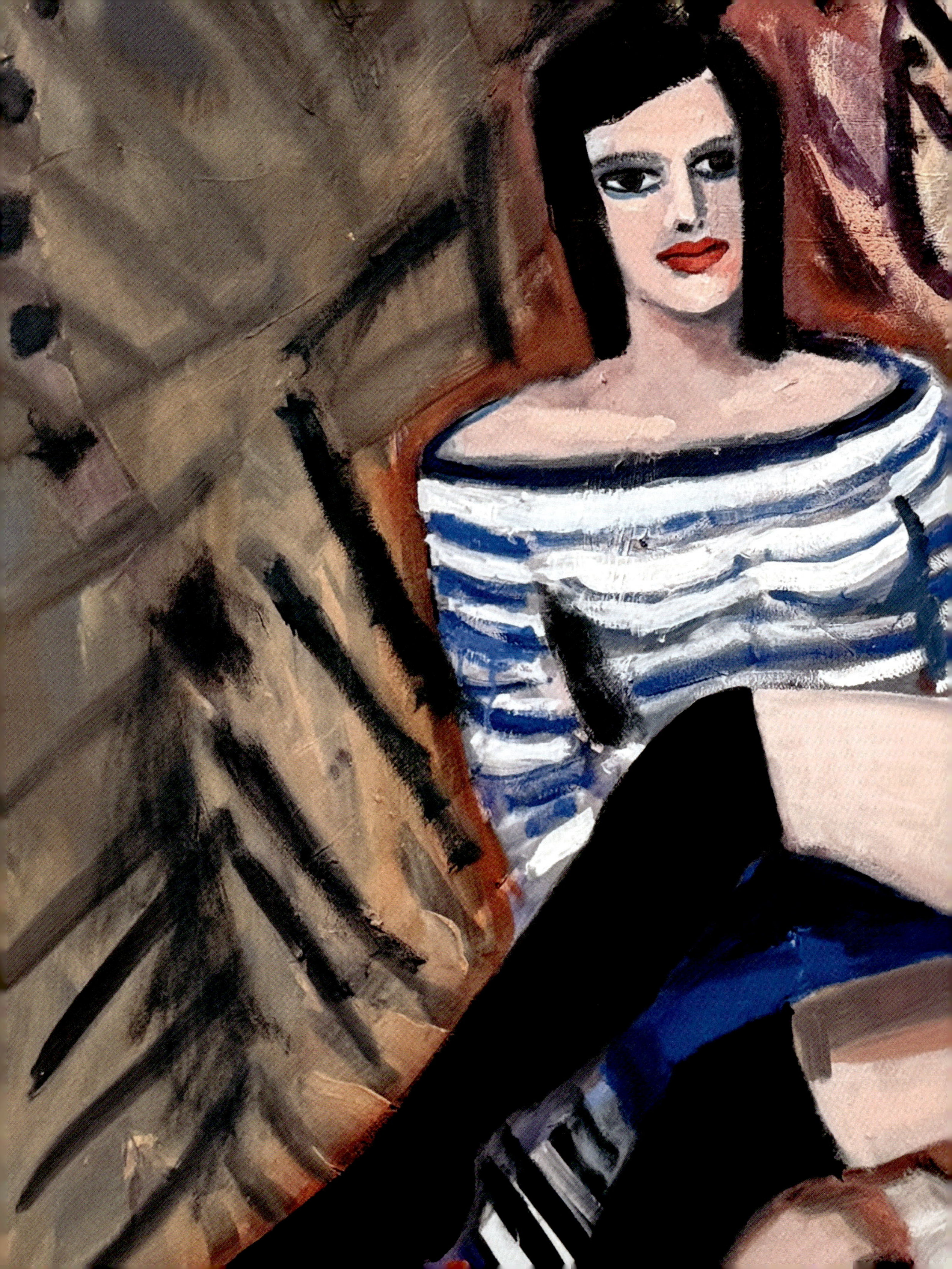

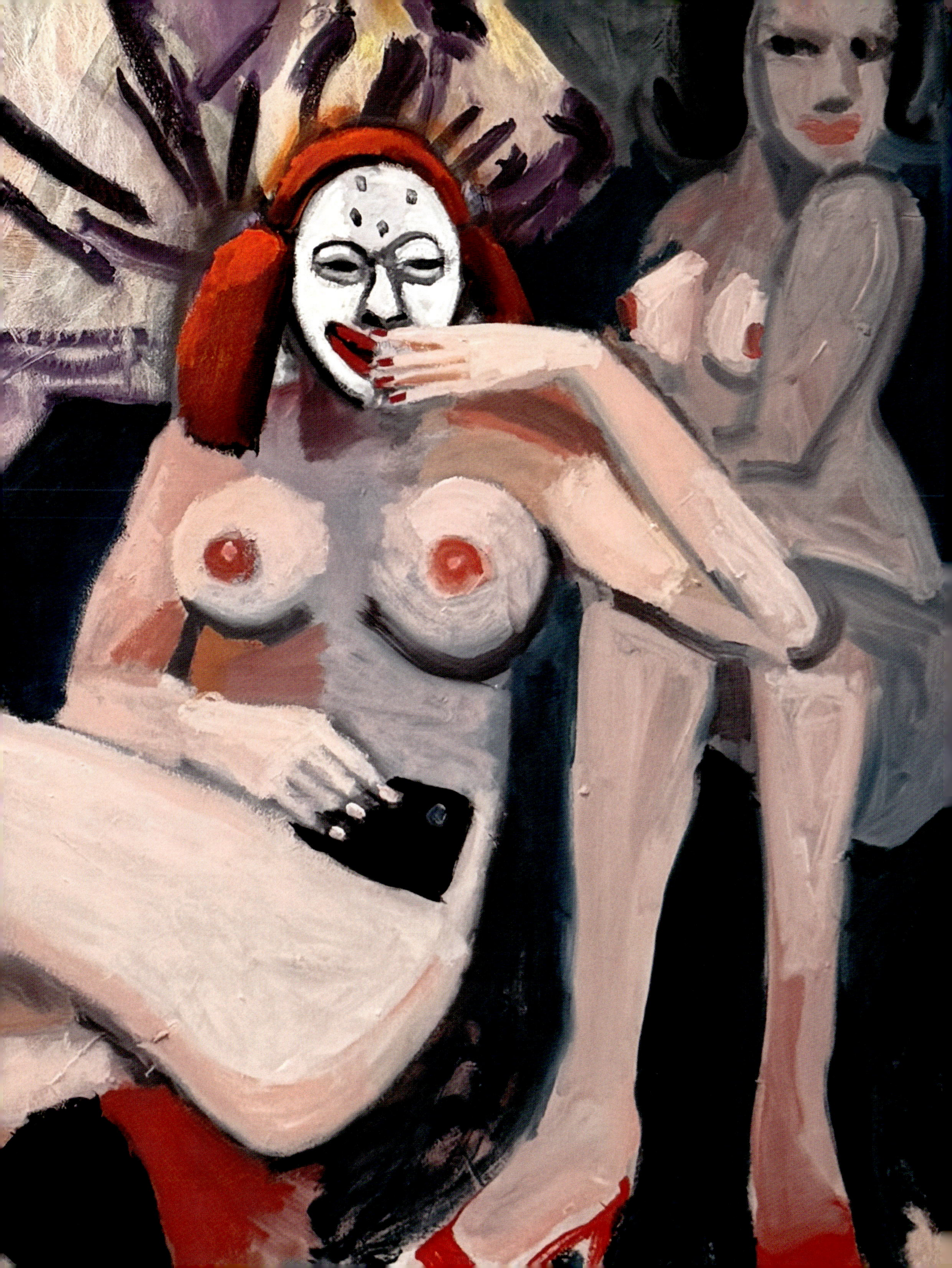

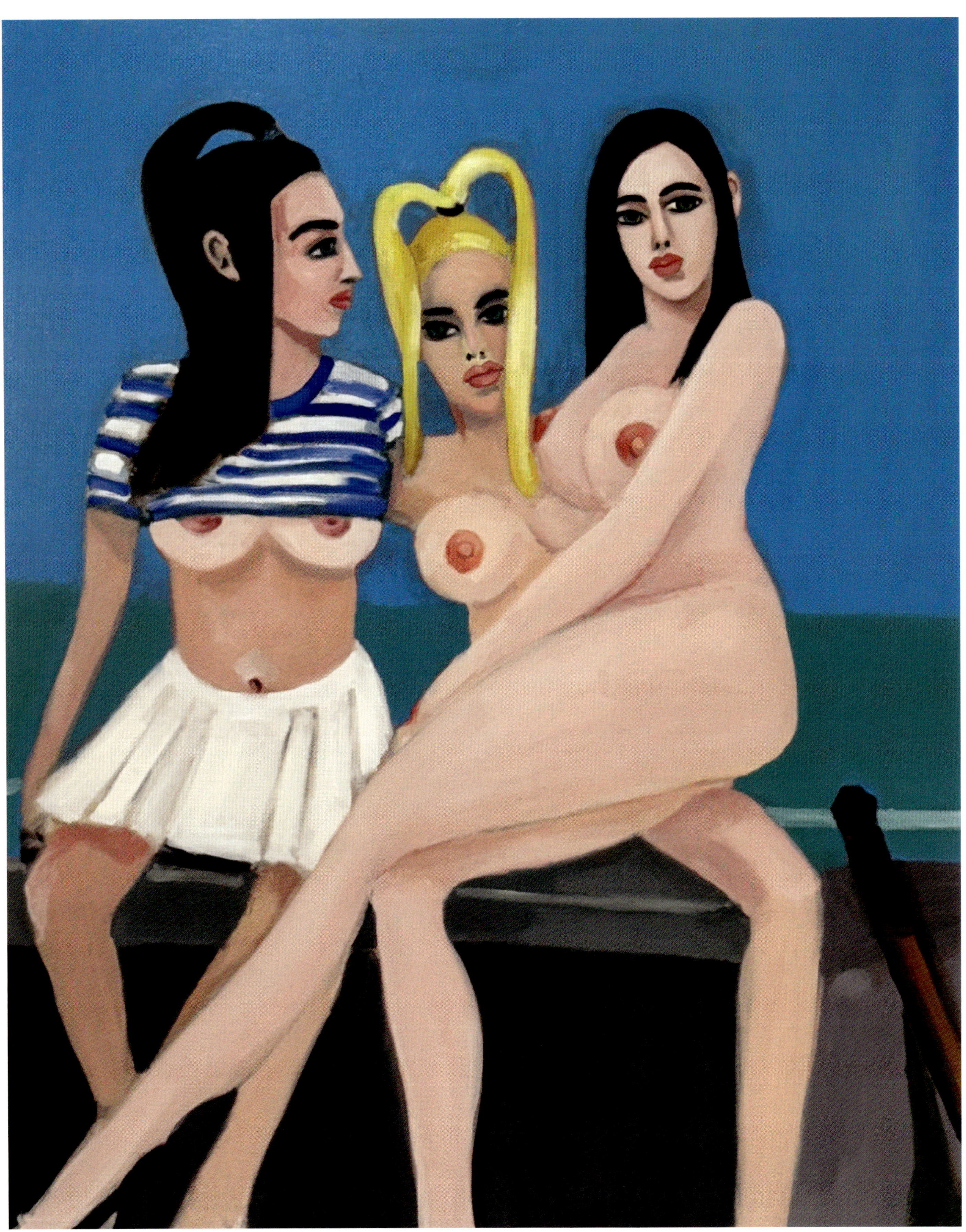

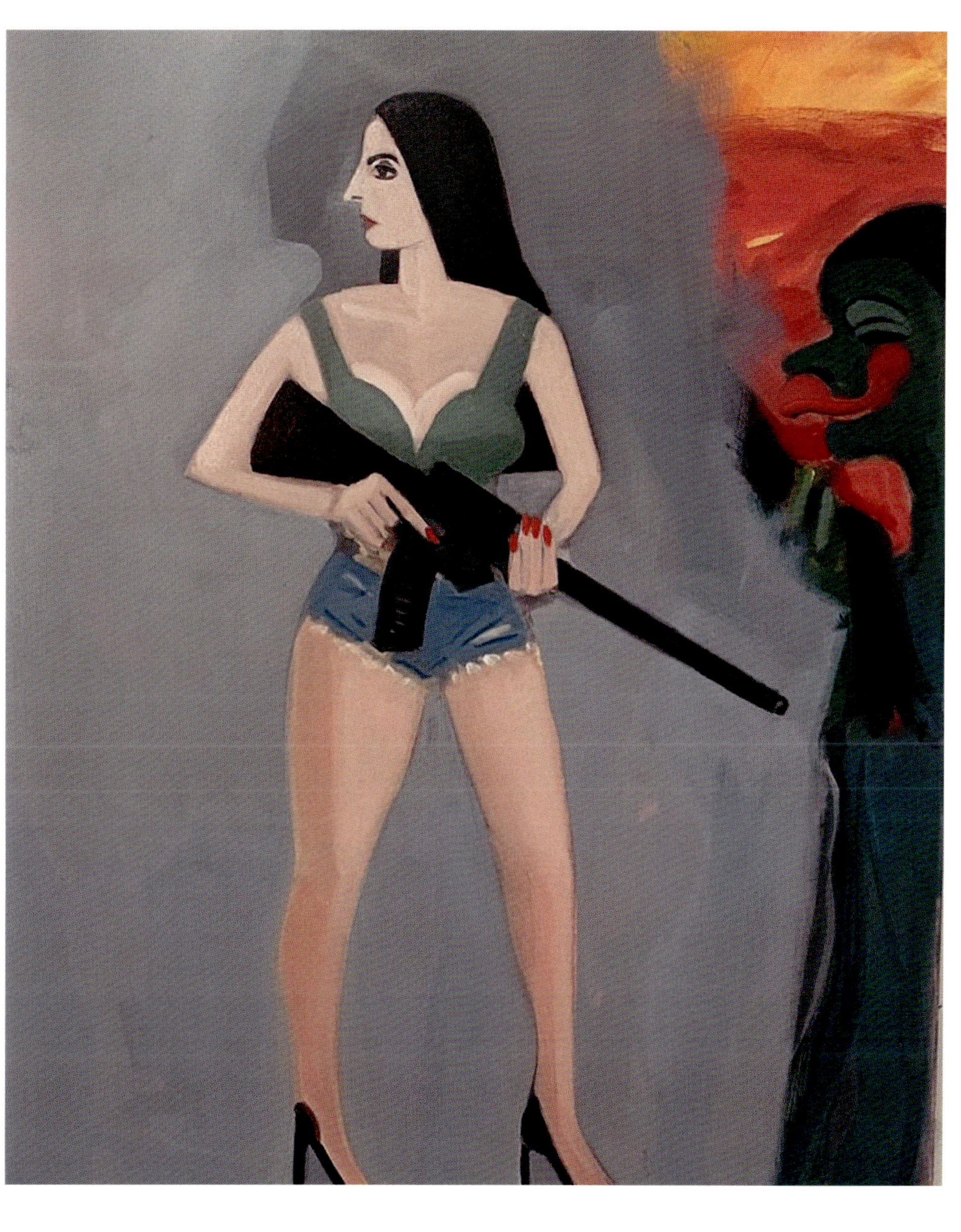

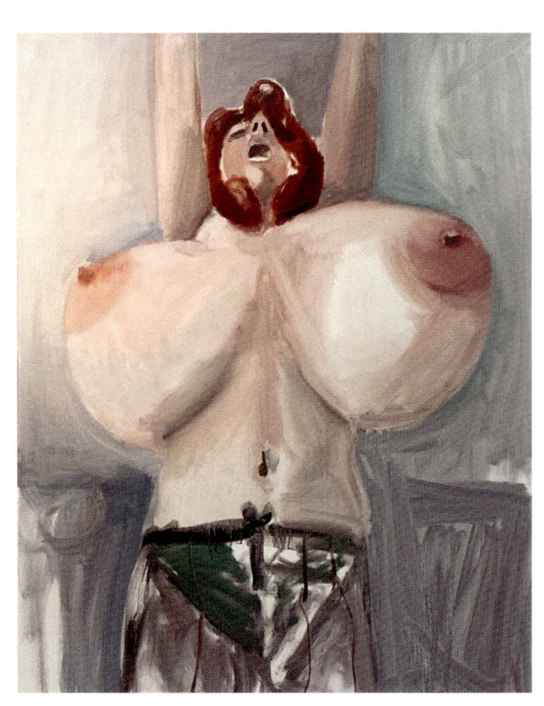

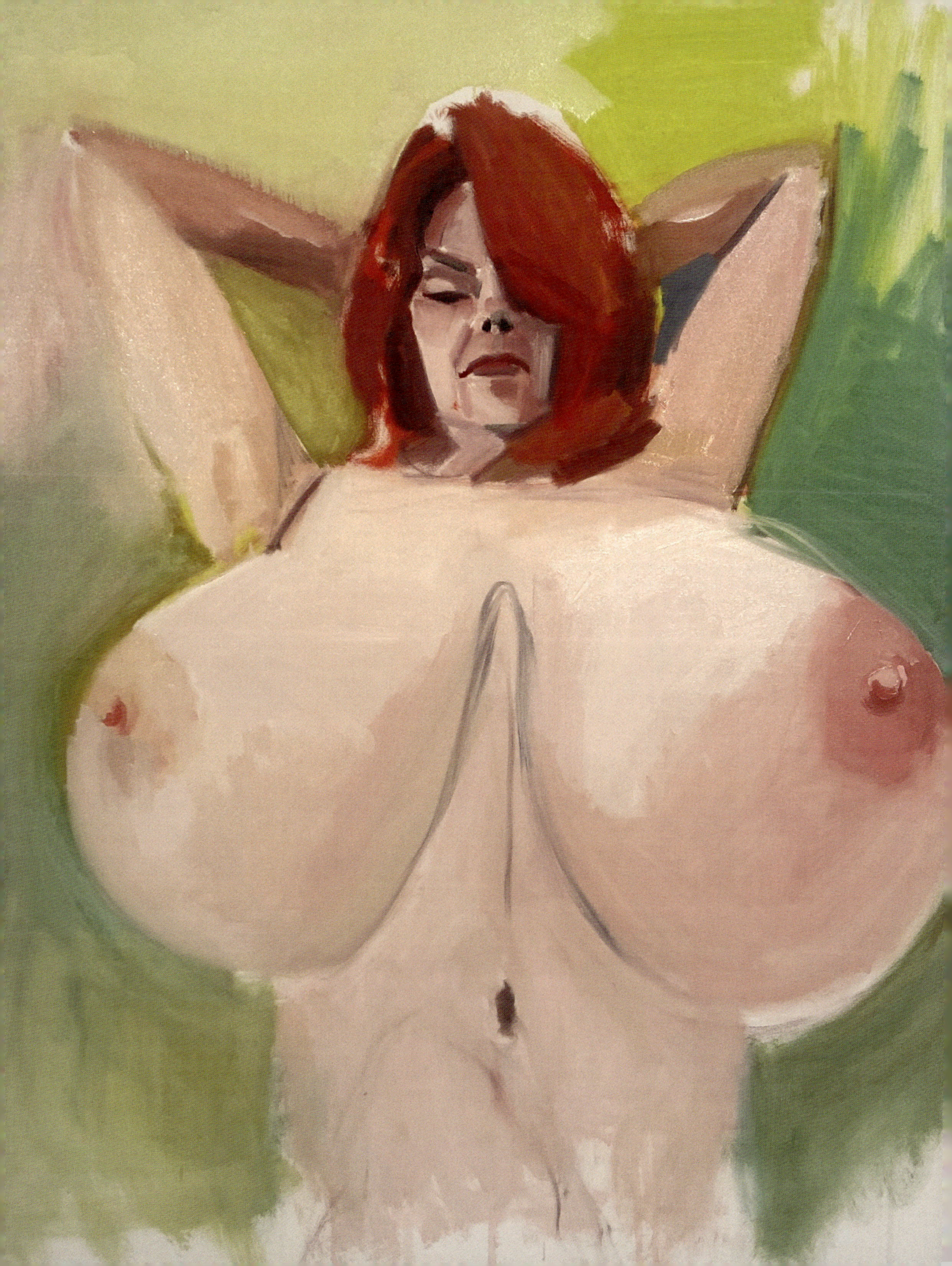

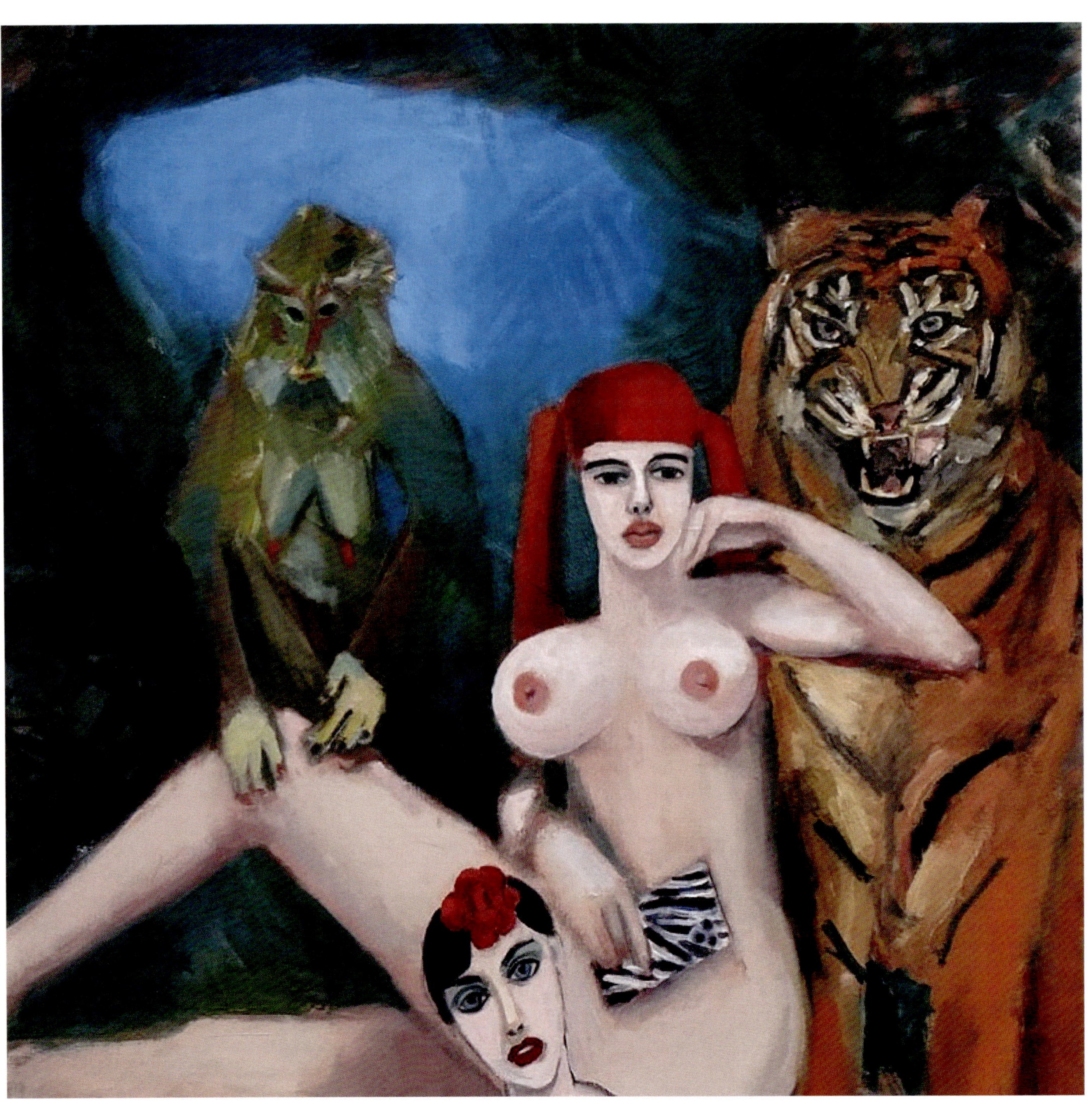

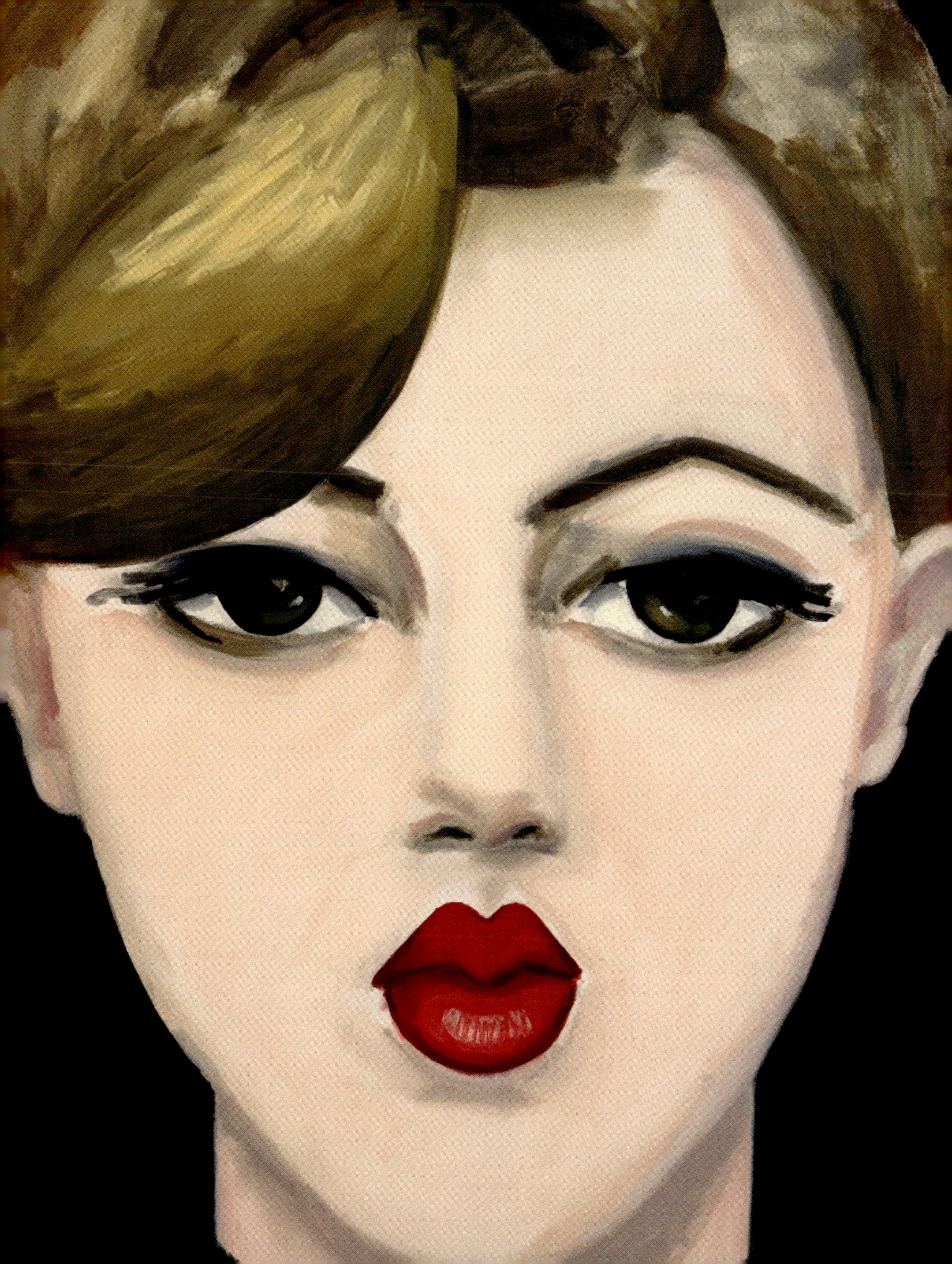

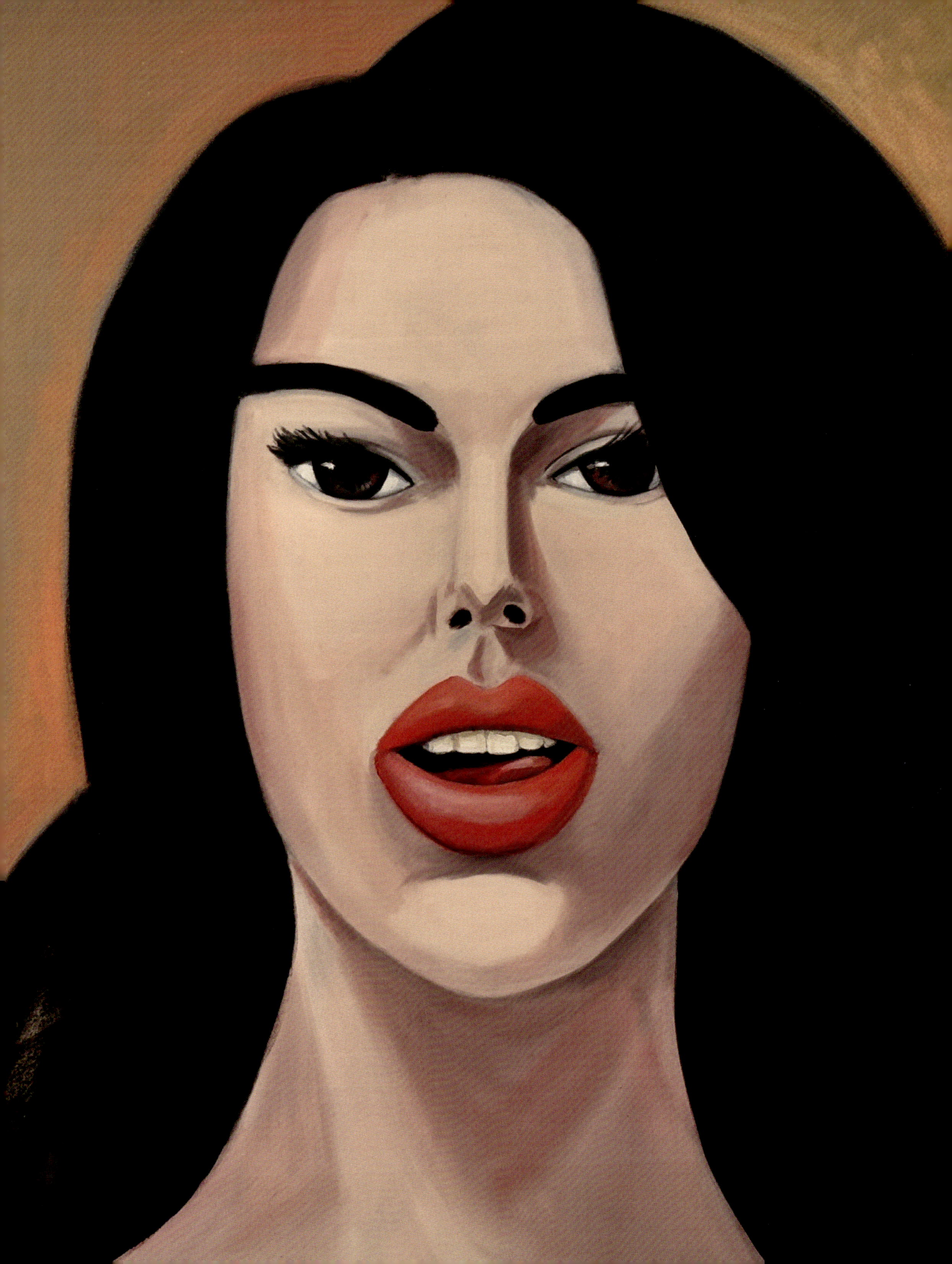

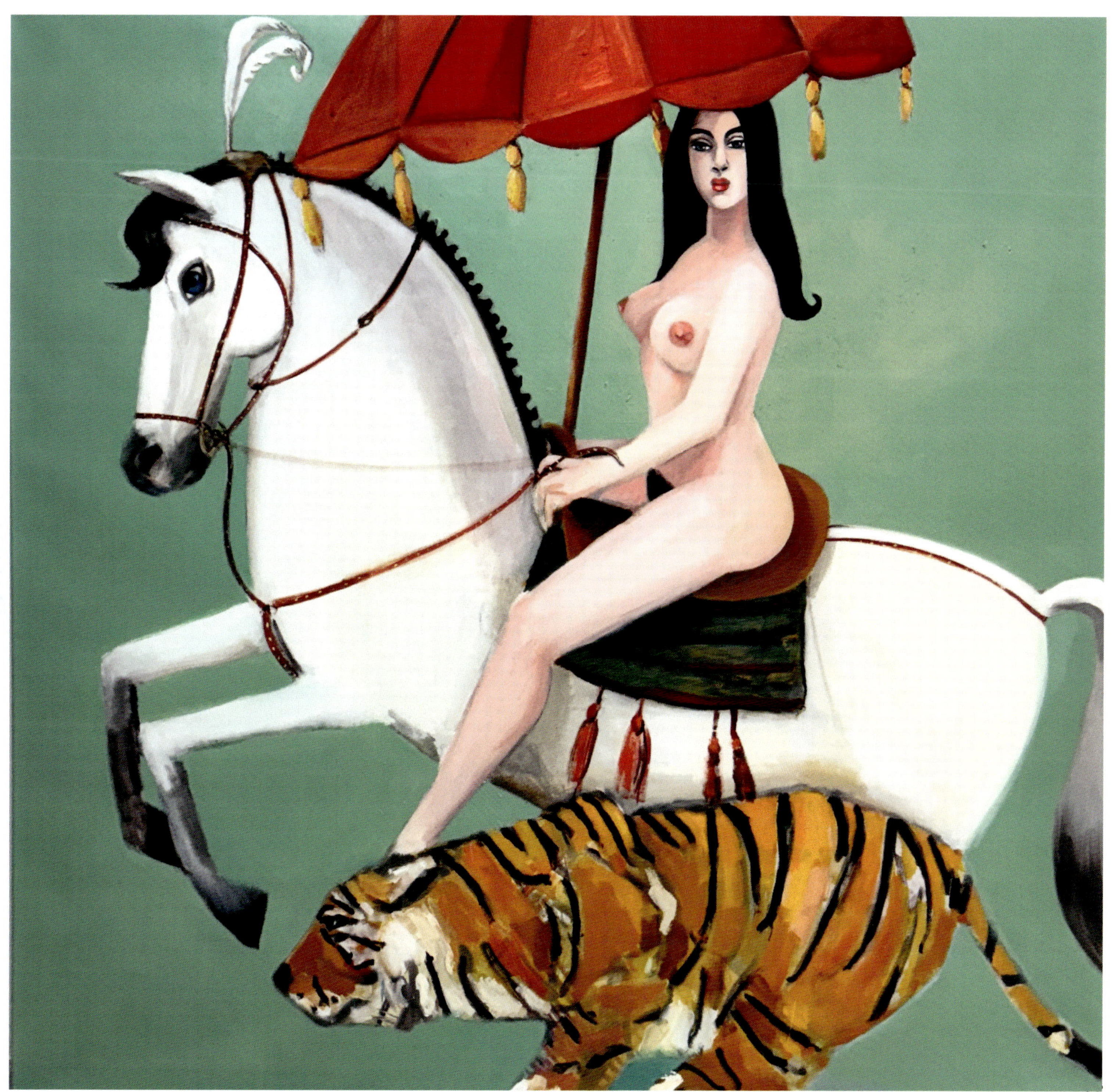

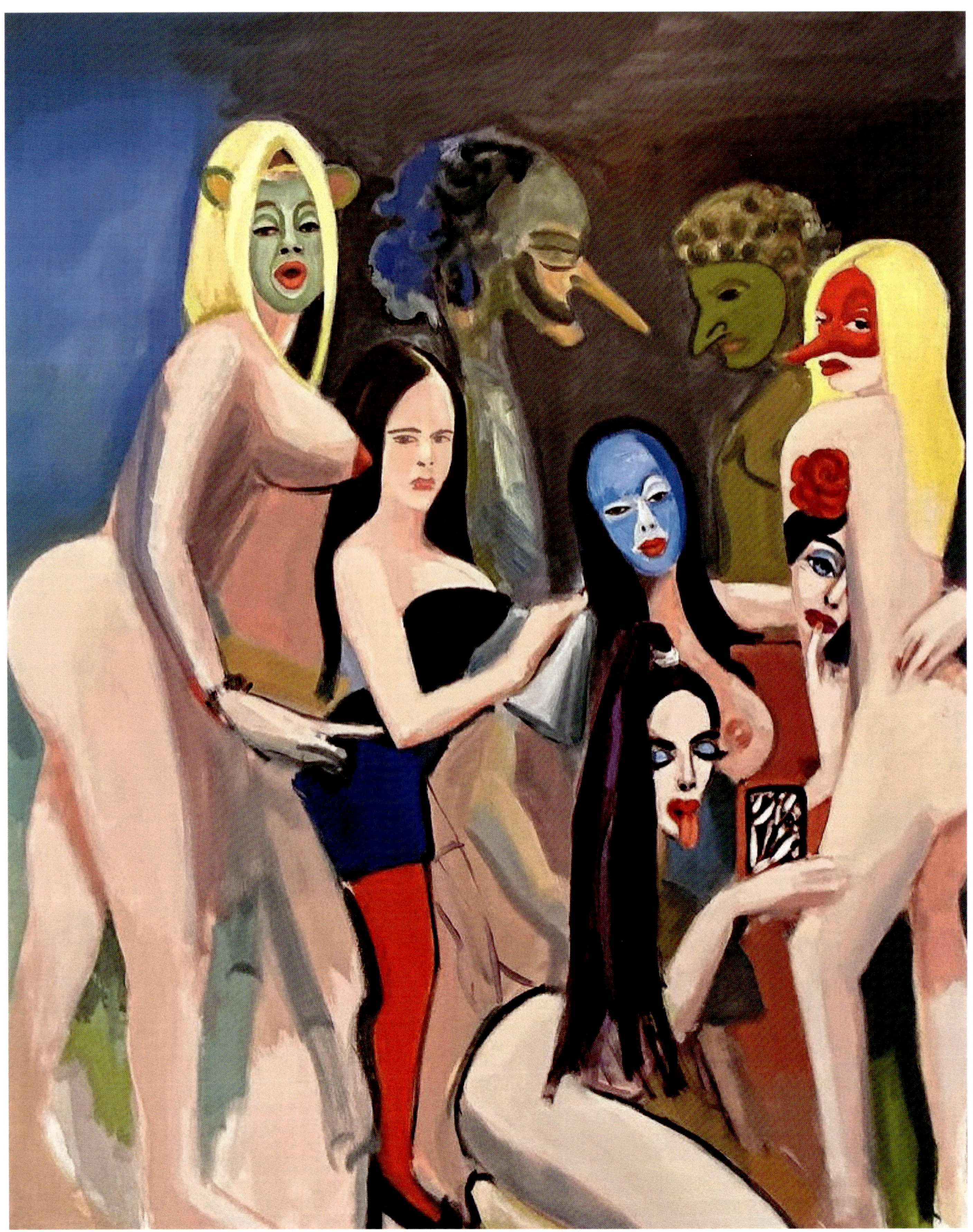

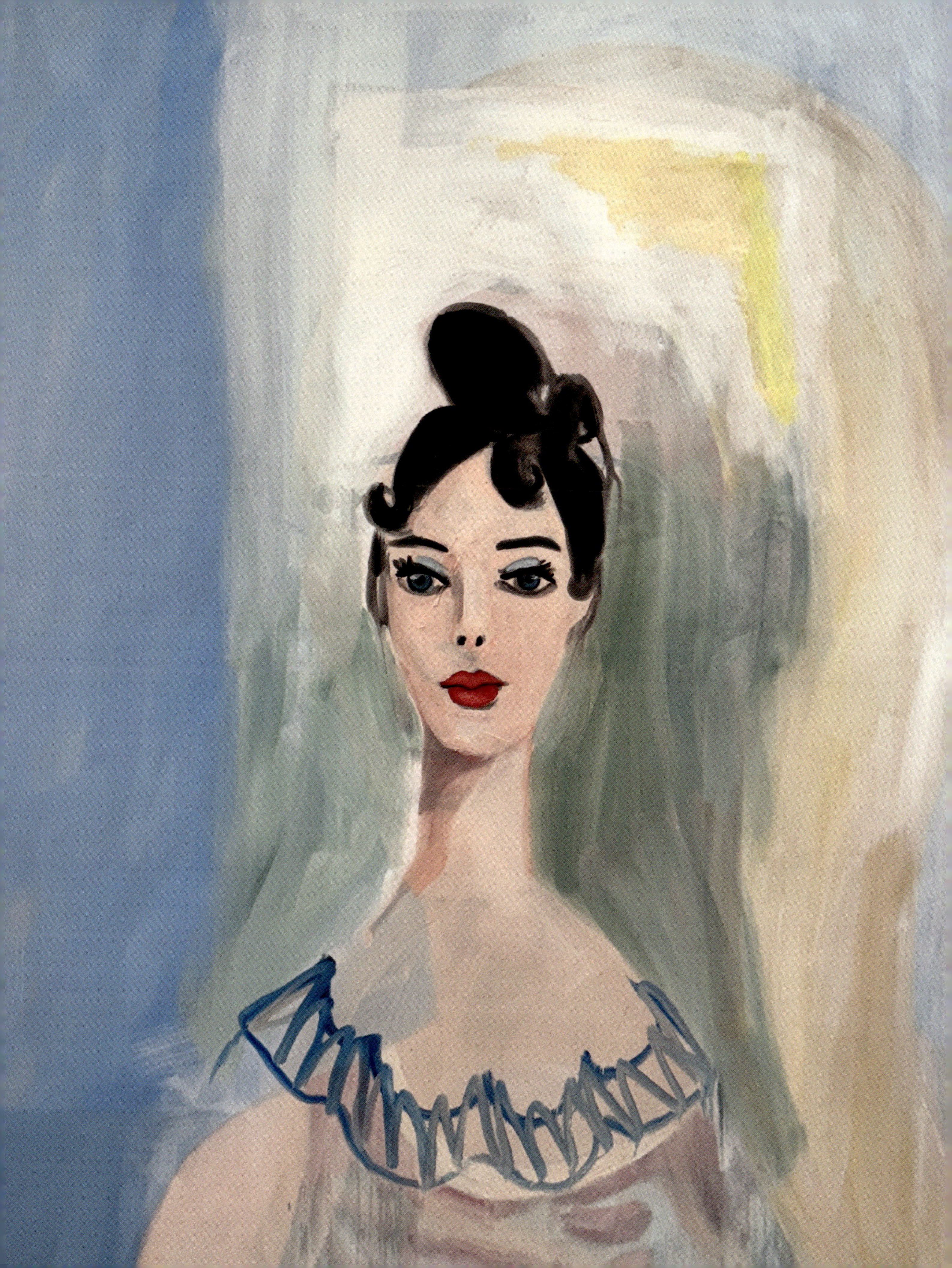

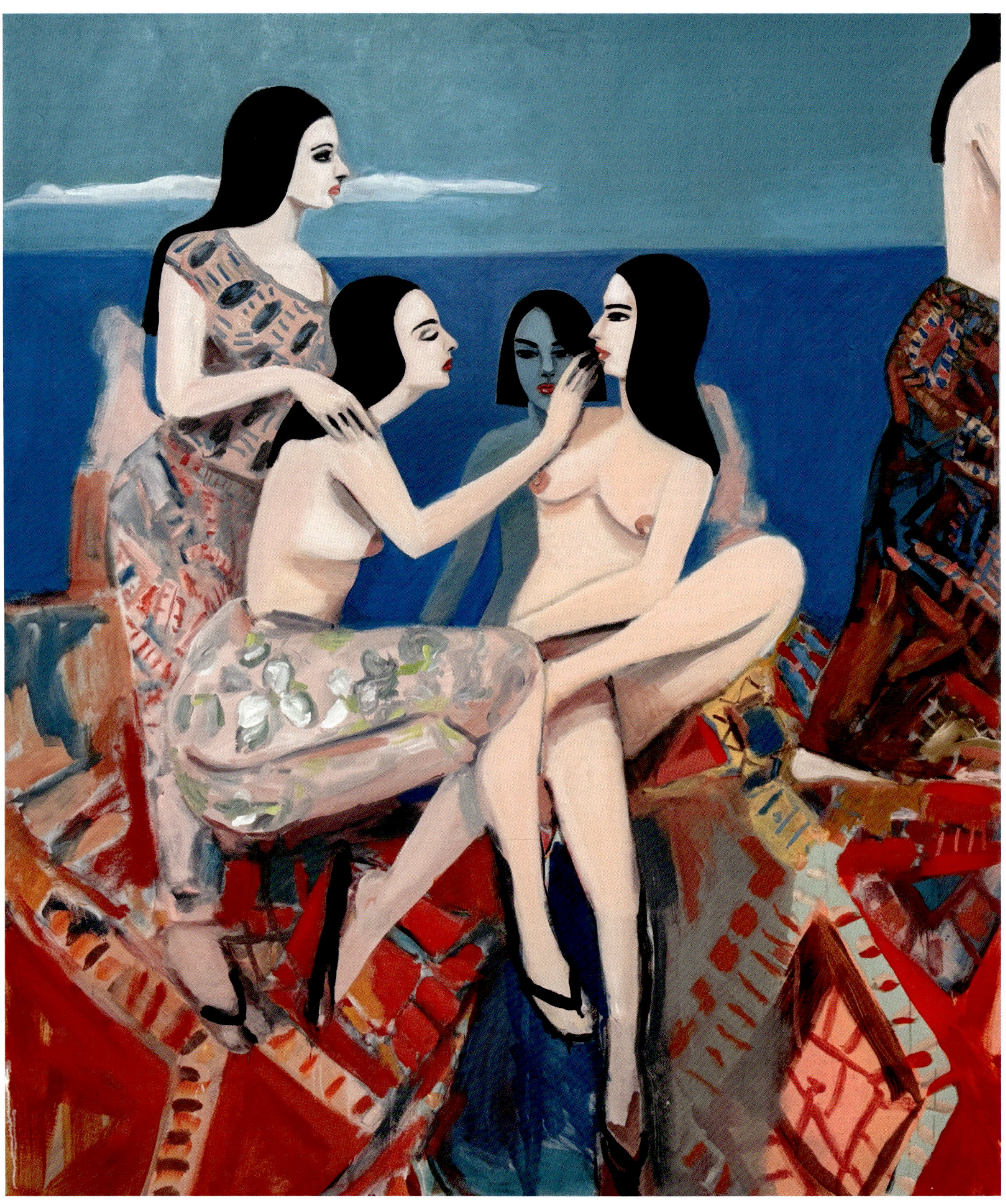

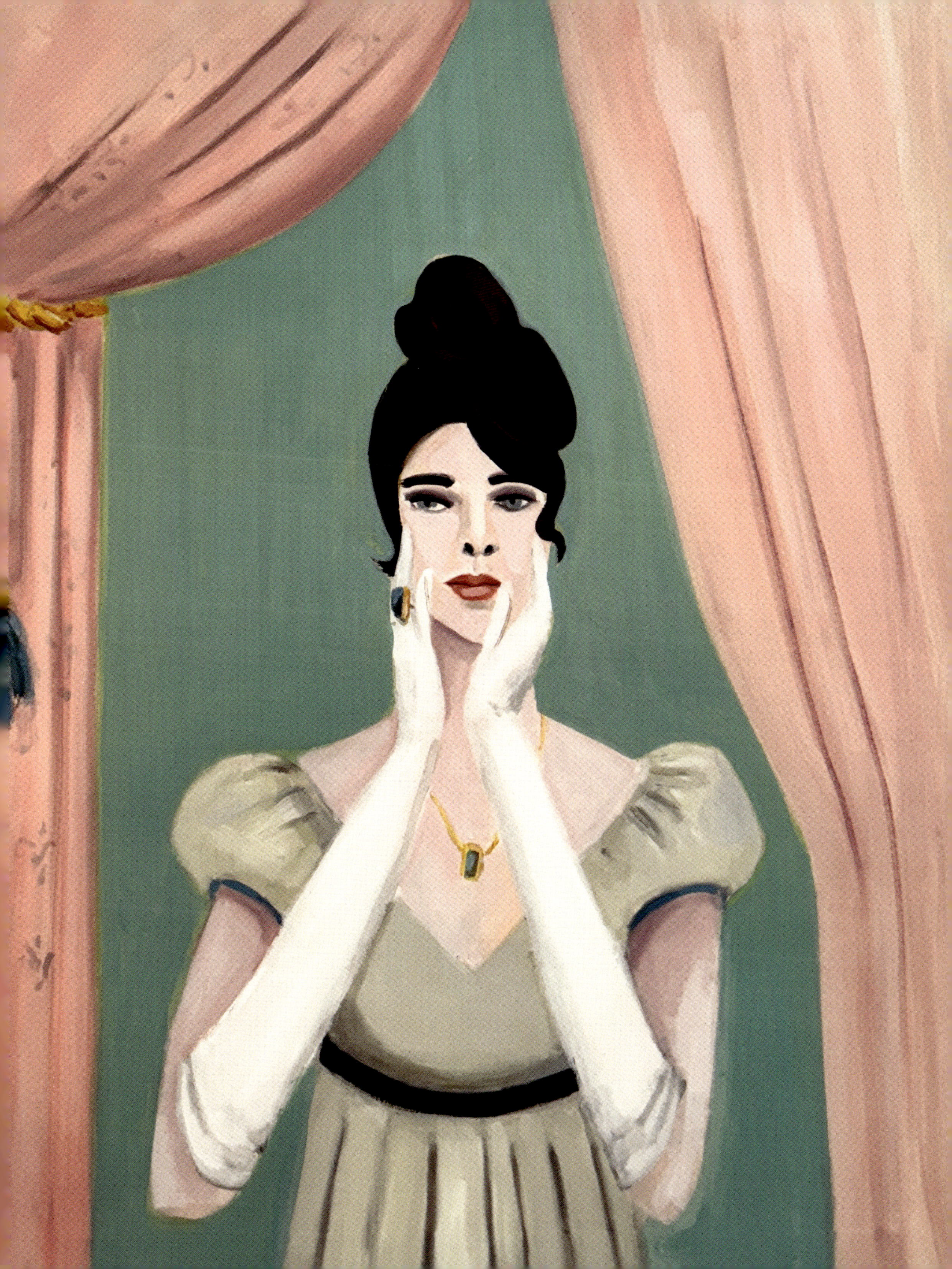

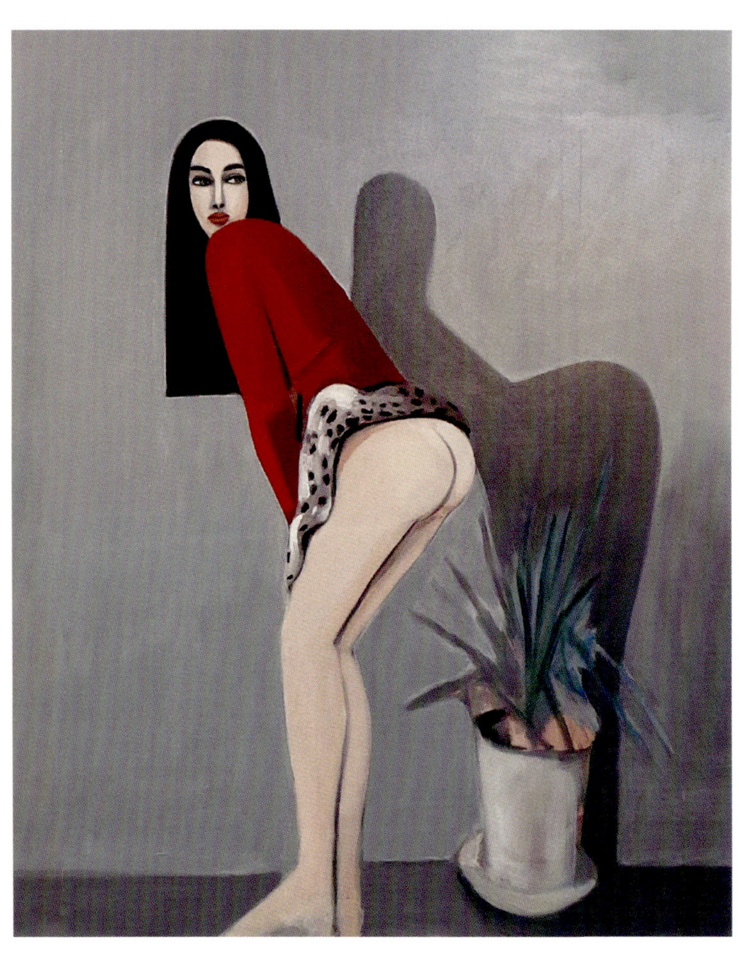

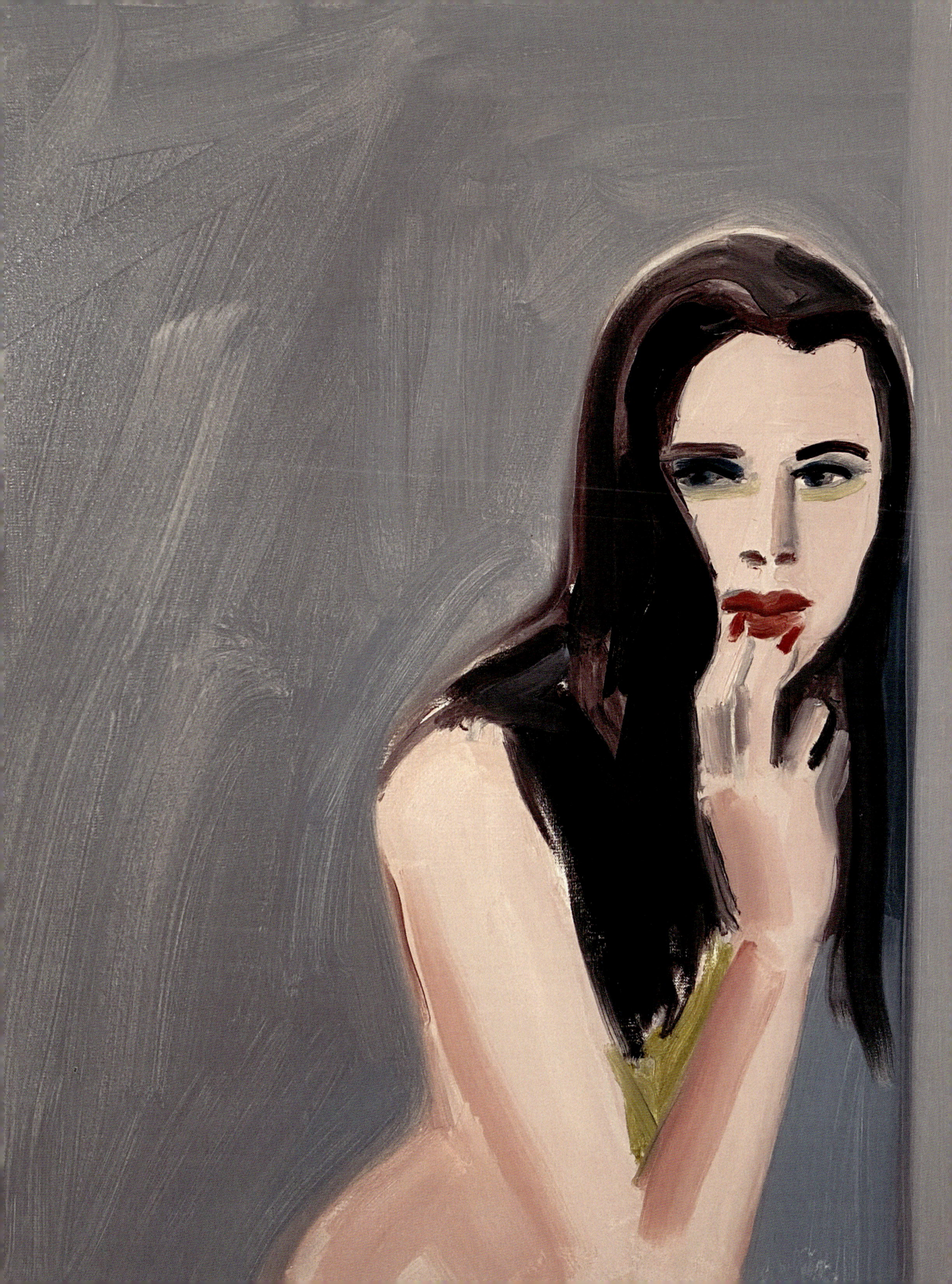

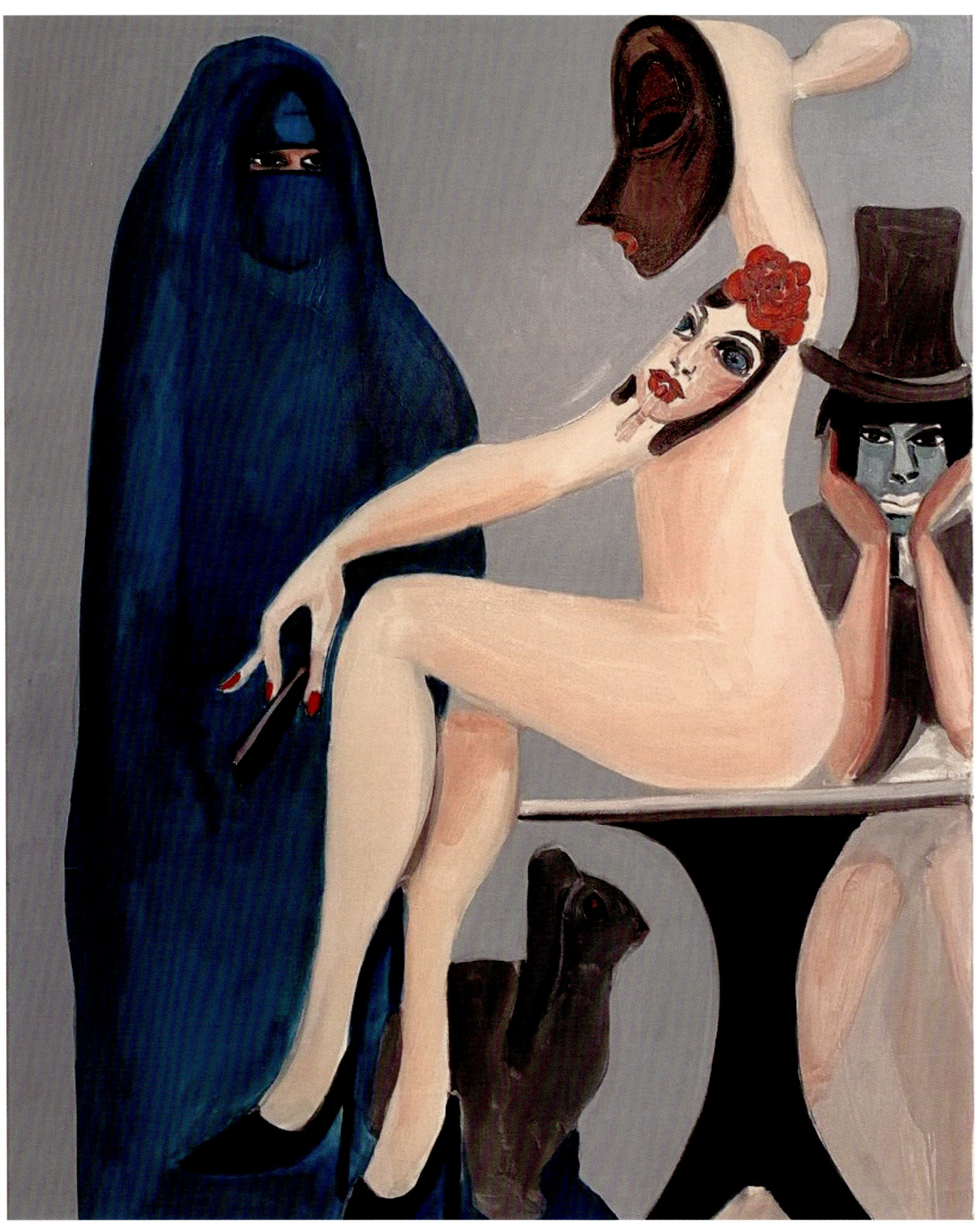

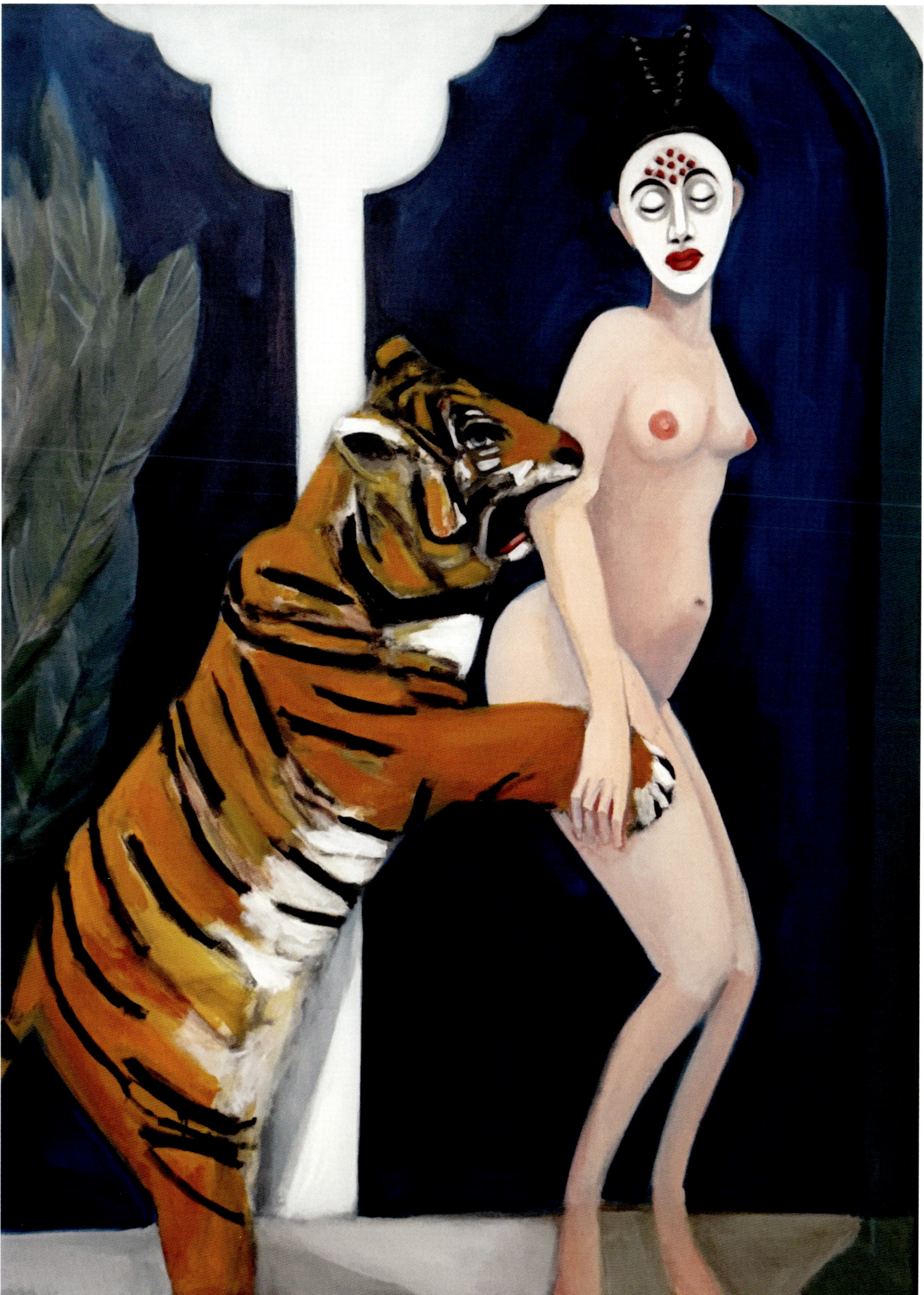

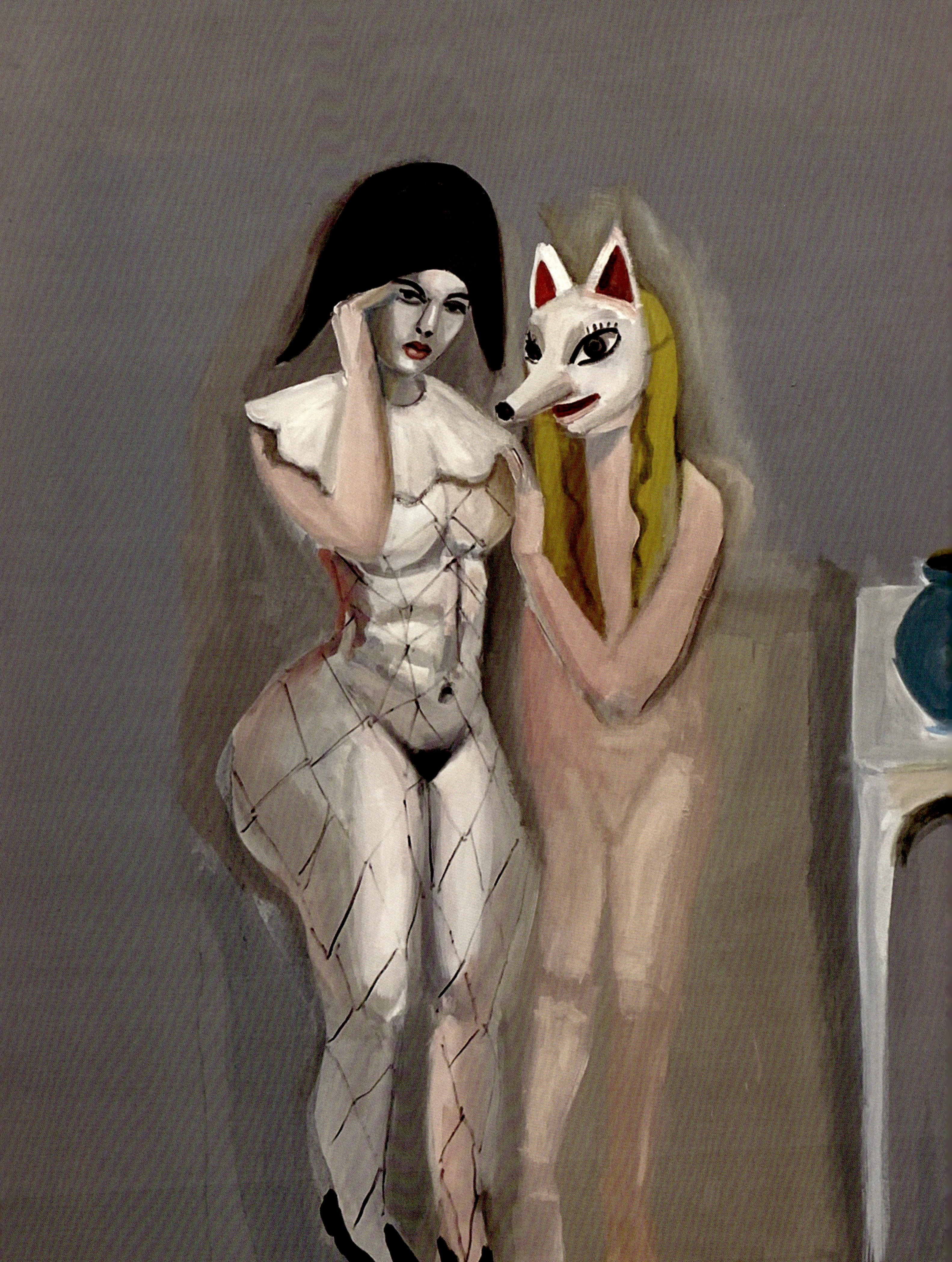

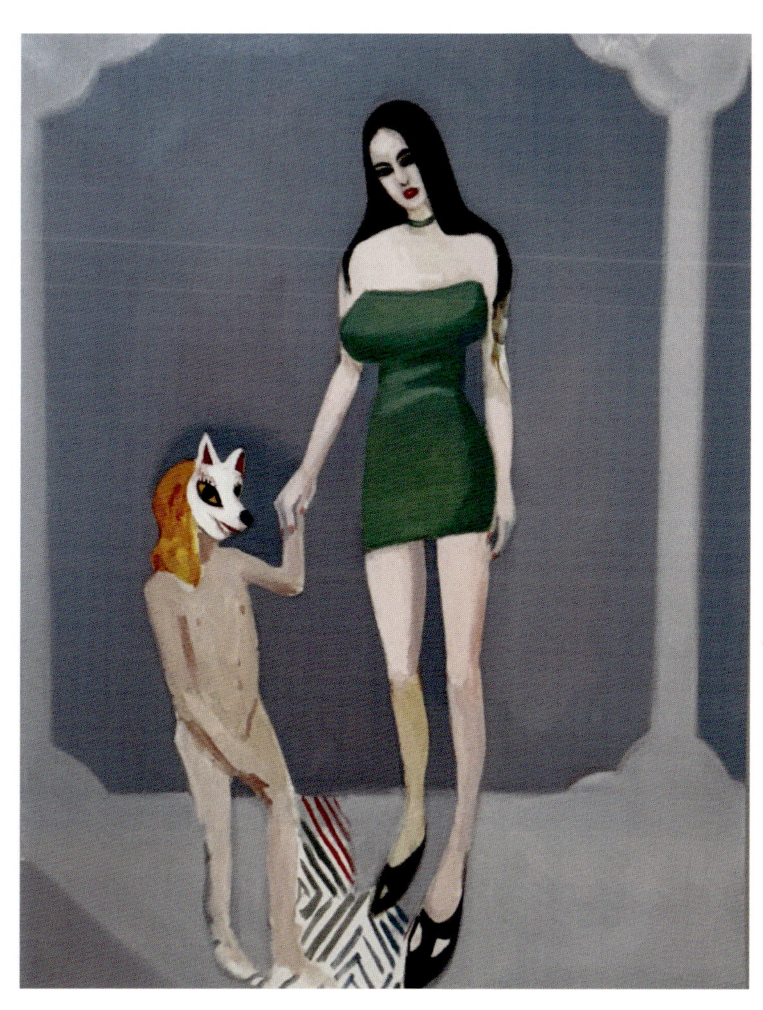

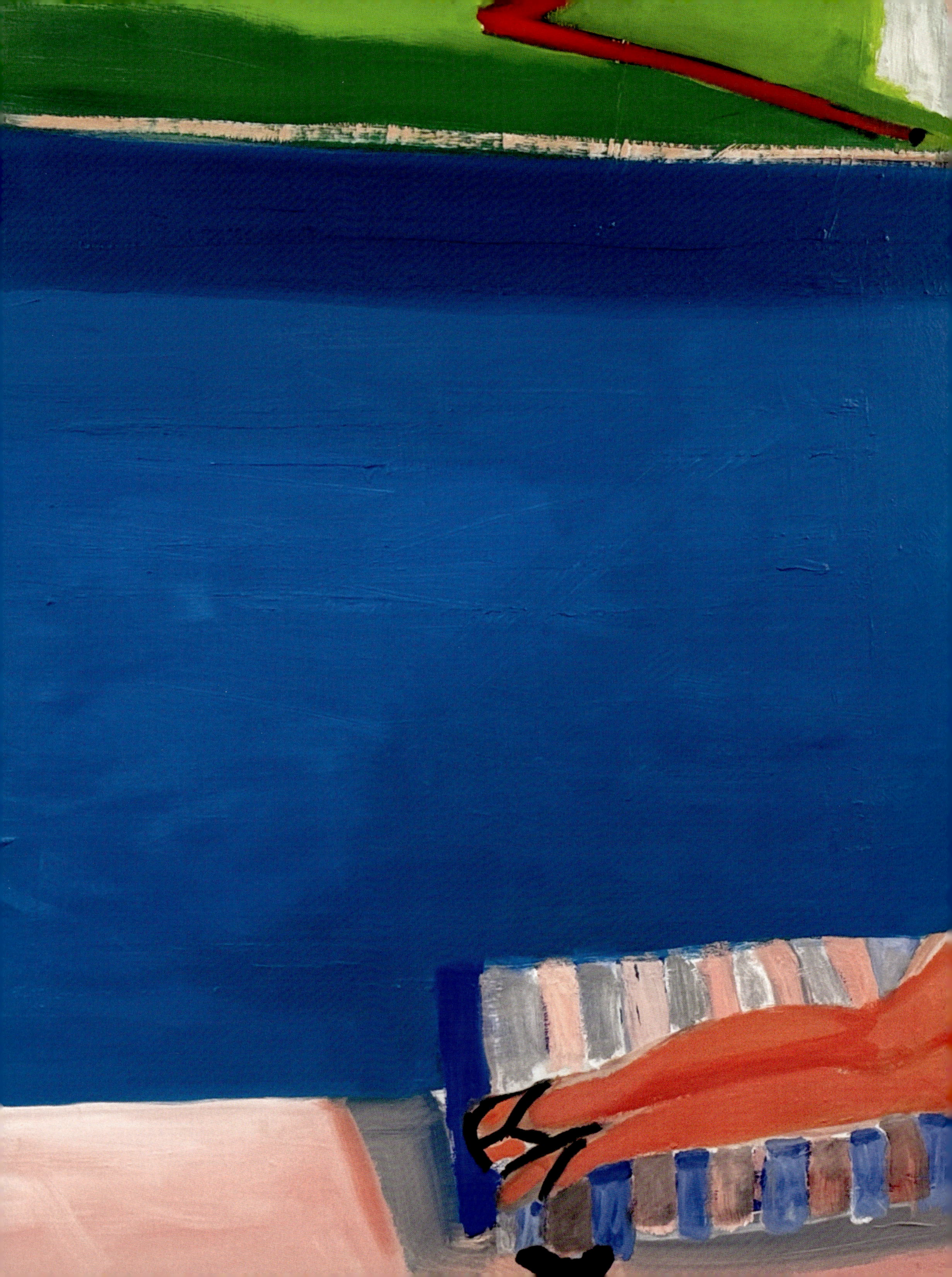

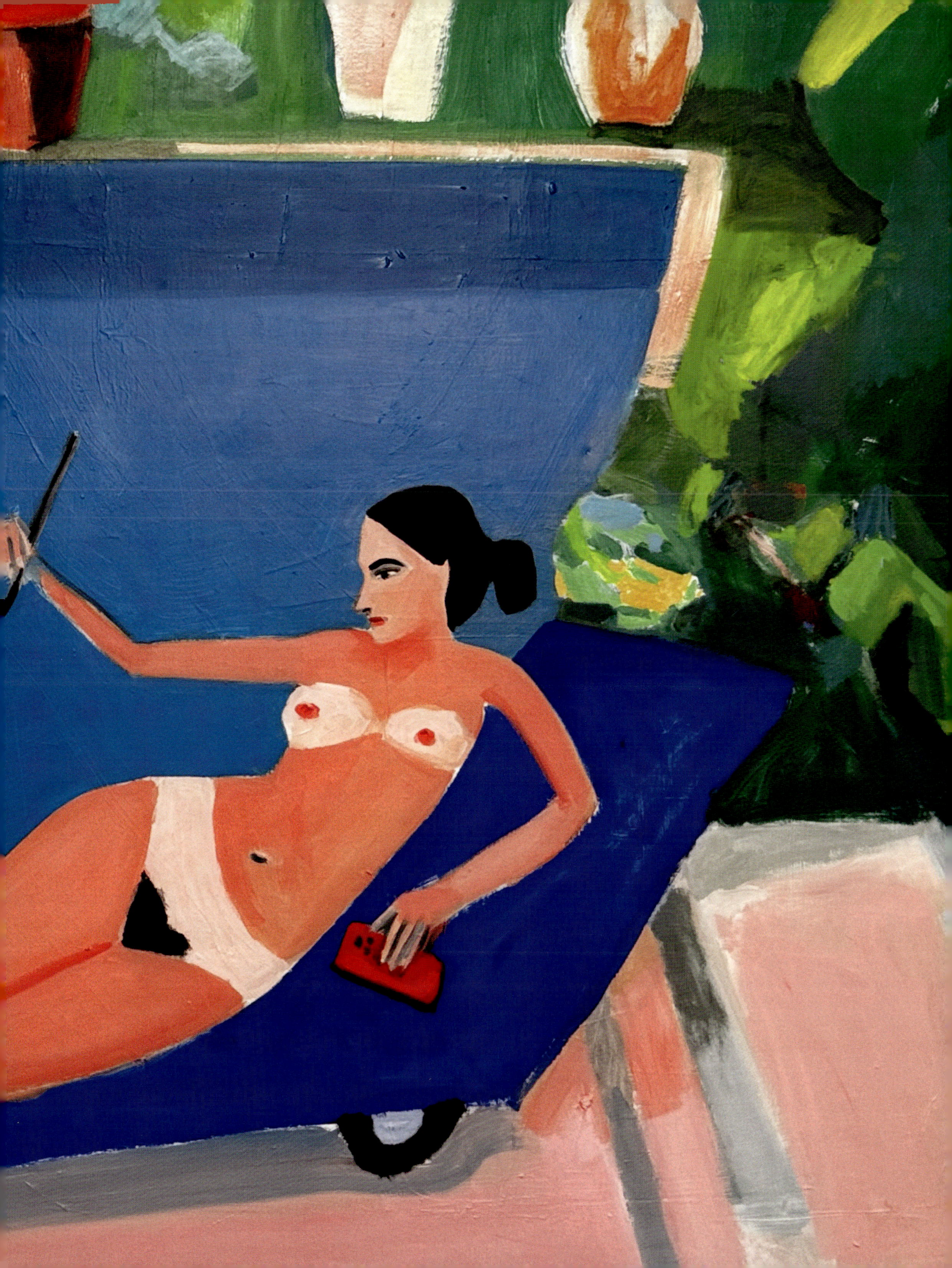

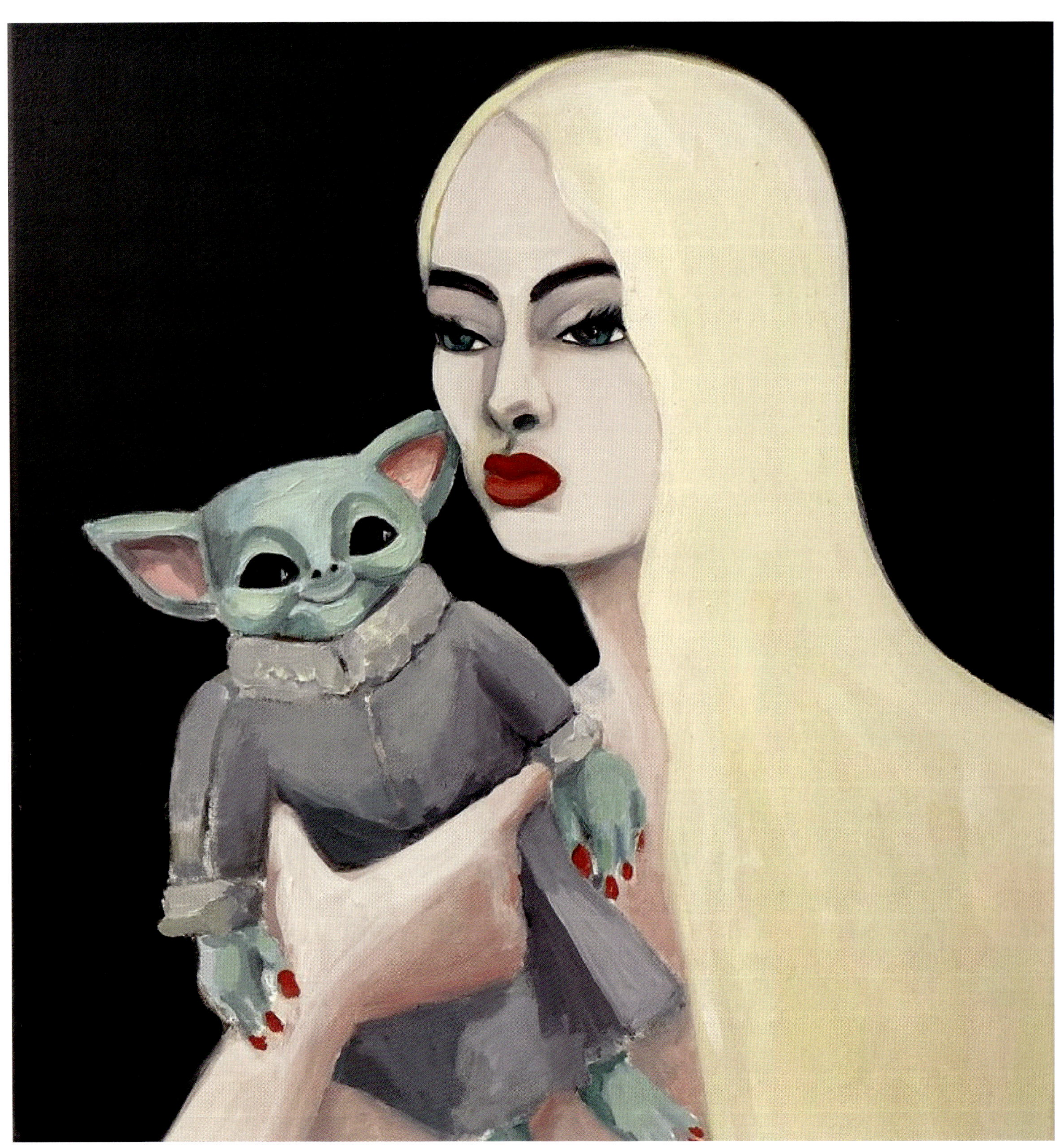

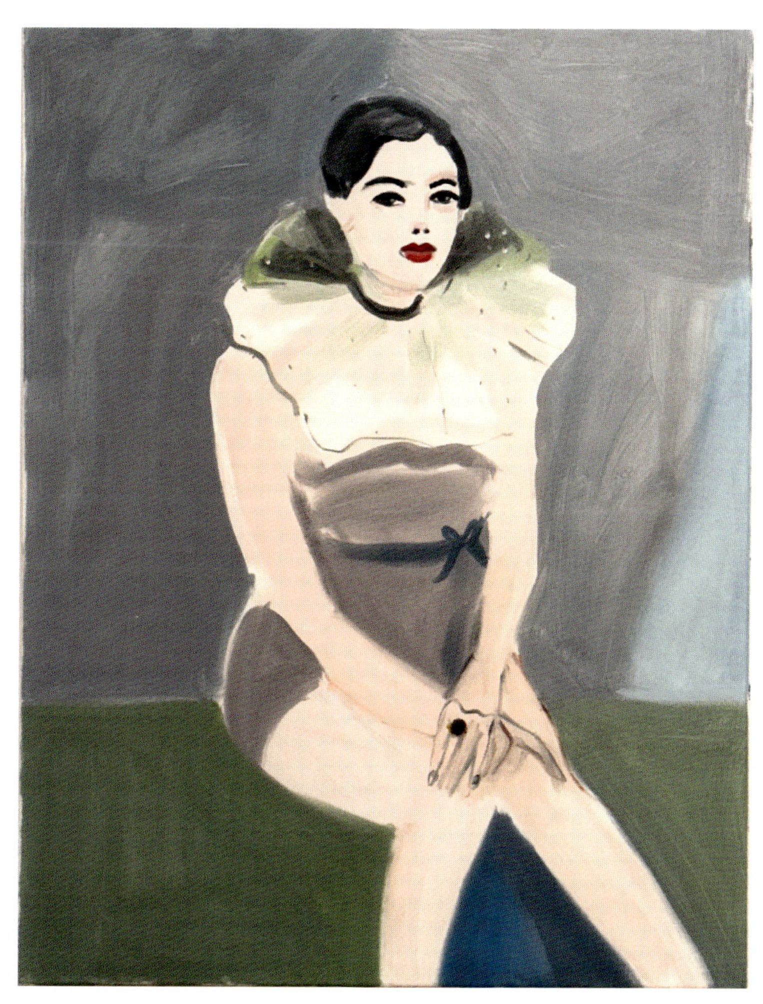

Index

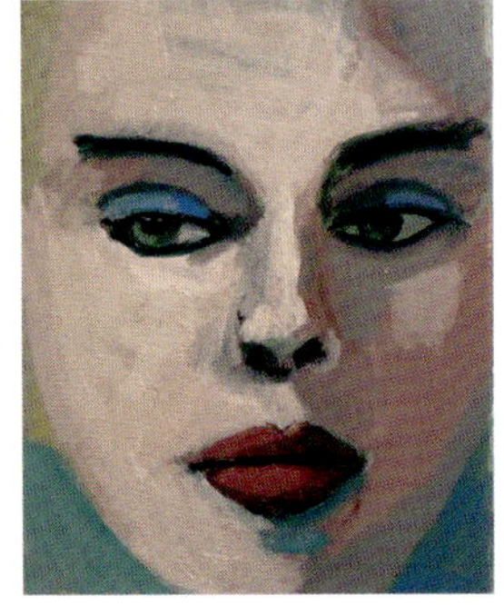

p. 2
Blue 2023
Oil on Canvas
14"×11"

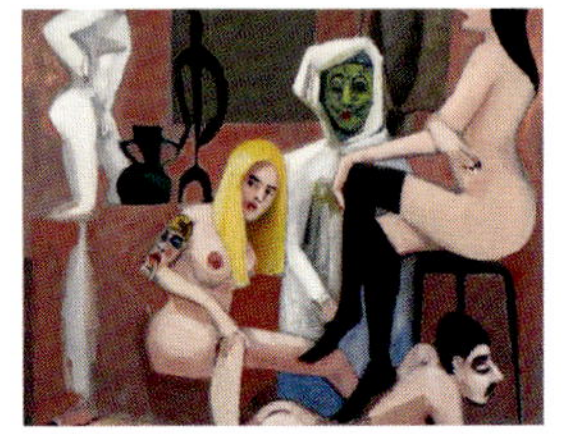

p. 3
The Collector 2022
Oil On Canvas
48"×48"

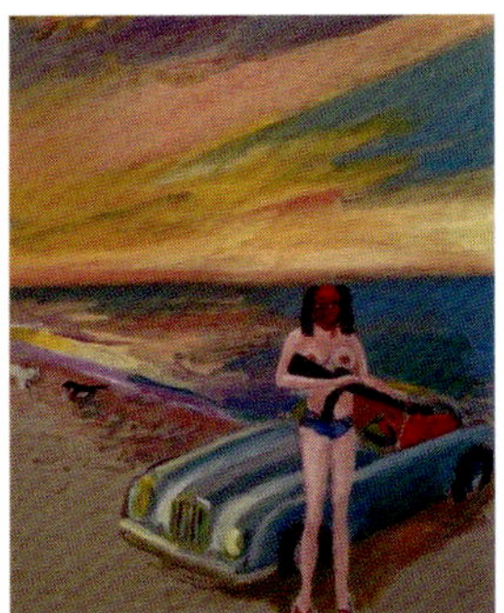

p. 4
Washed Up 2023
Oil on Canvas
48"×36"

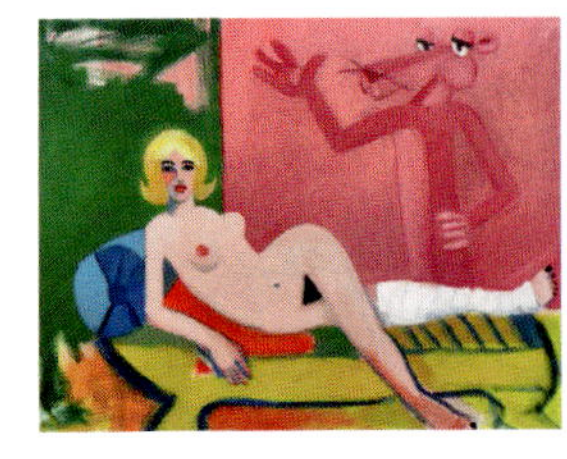

p. 5
Mother 2024
Oil on Canvas
64"×48"

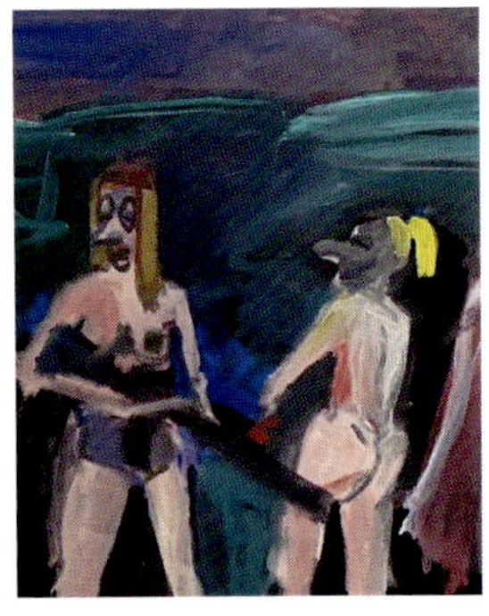

p. 6
Girls w Guns 2022
Oil On Canvas
48"×36"

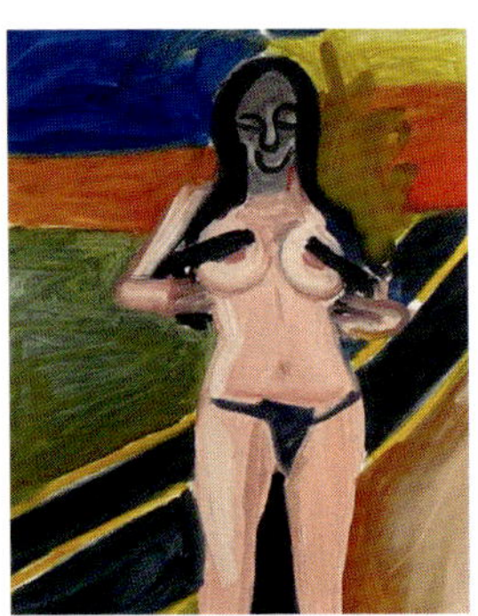

p. 7
Girl With Gun 2022
Oil On Canvas
48"×36"

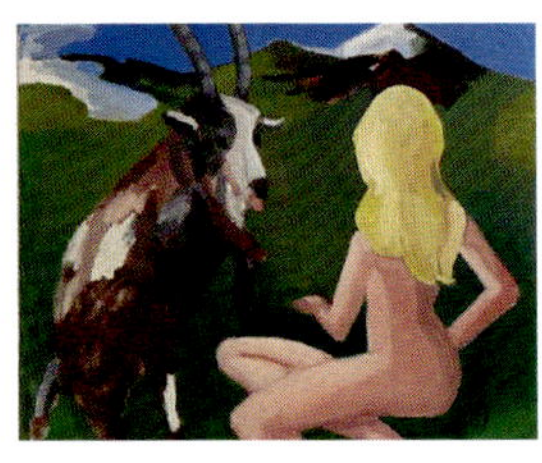

pp. 8–9
Love Land Pass 2022
Oil on Canvas
34"×34"

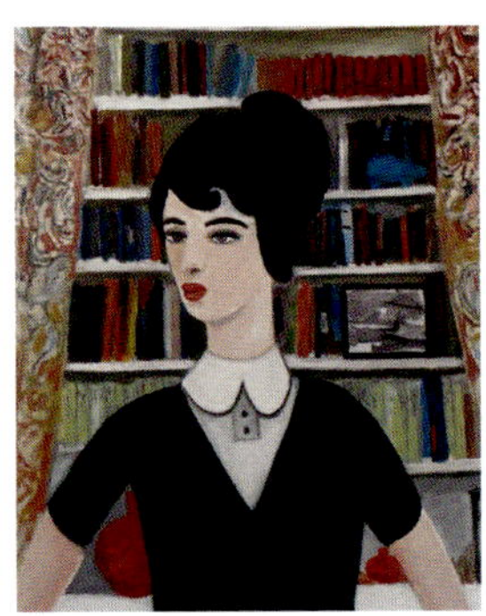

p. 10
The Library 2024
Oil on Canvas
40"×30"

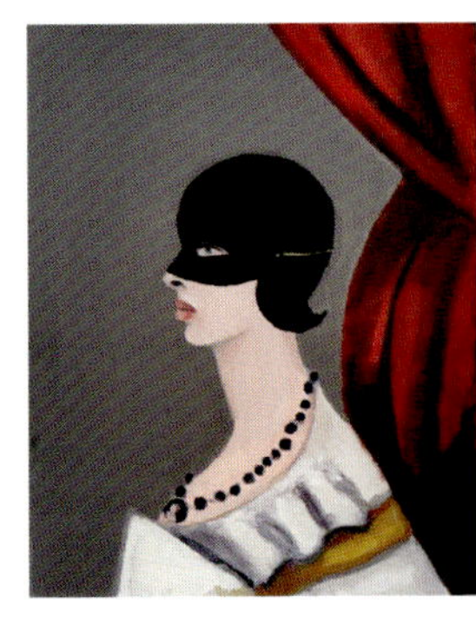

p. 11
Federal Portrait 2024
Oil on Canvas
16"×14"

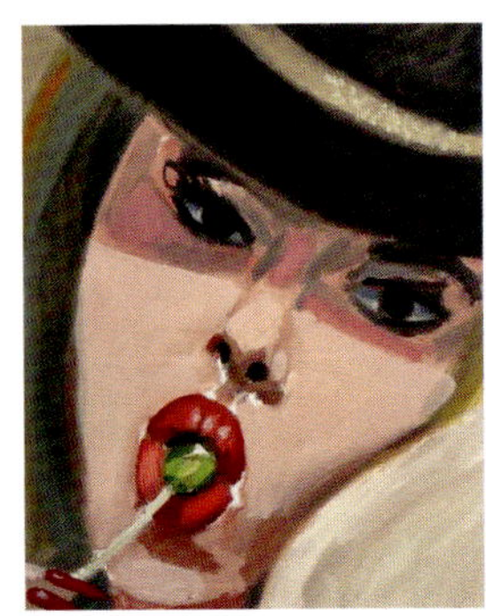

p. 12
Sucker Green 2023
Oil on Canvas
20"×18"

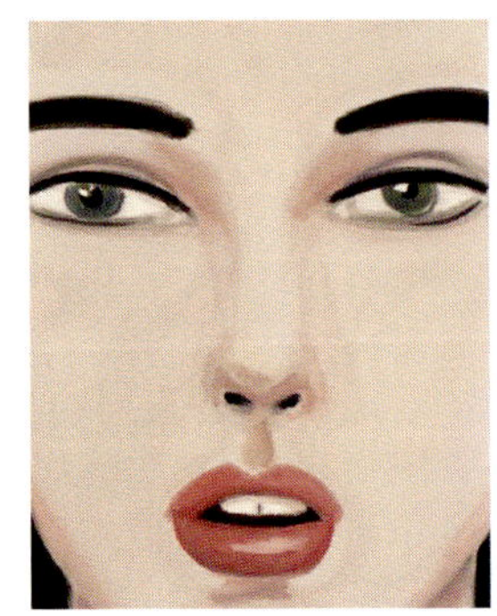

p. 13
Green Eyes 2023
Oil On Canvas
36"×36"

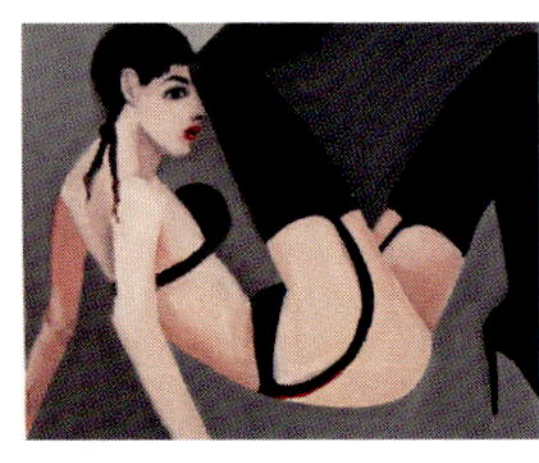

p. 14–15
Cover Girl 2024
Oil on Canvas
36"×24"

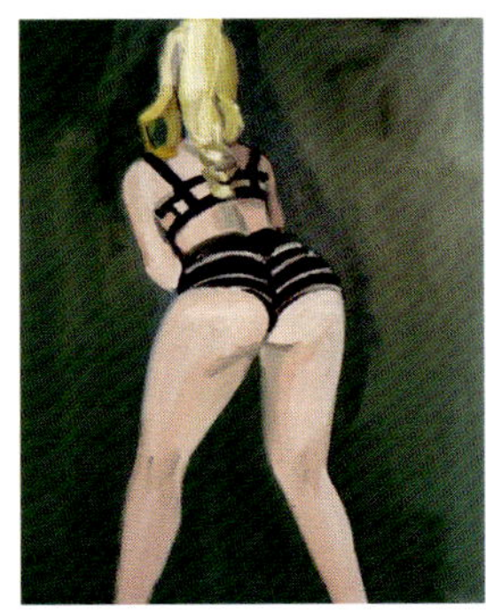

p. 16
Backside 2024
Oil on Canvas
22"×18"

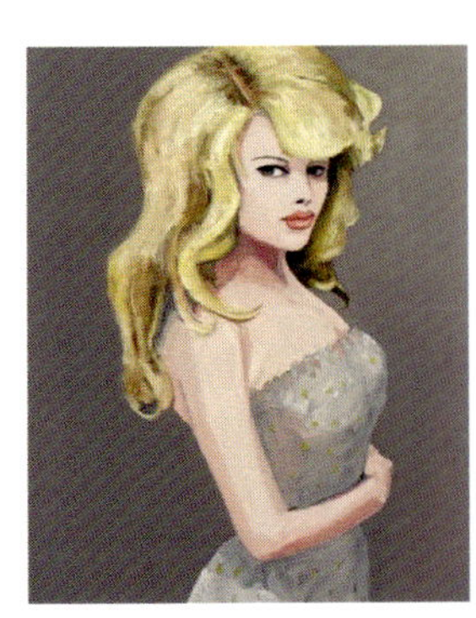

p. 17
Charo 2023
Oil on Canvas
40"×30"

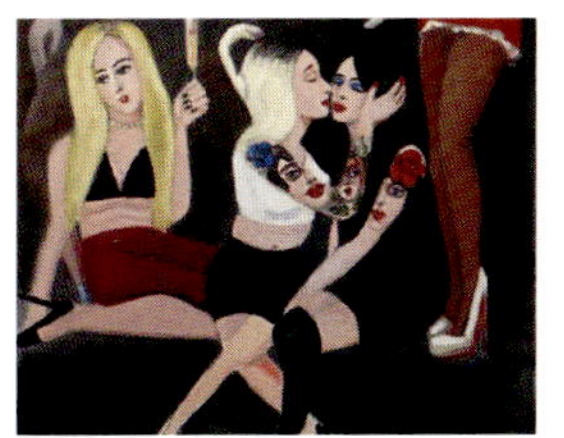

p. 18
Happy Hour 2023
Oil on Canvas
48"×48"

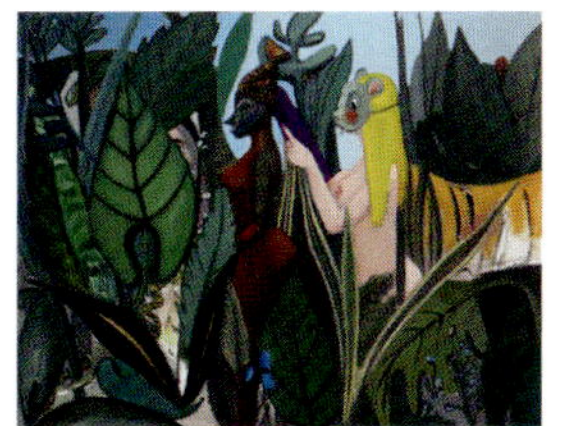

p. 19
Jungle Love 2022
Oil on Canvas
64"×48"

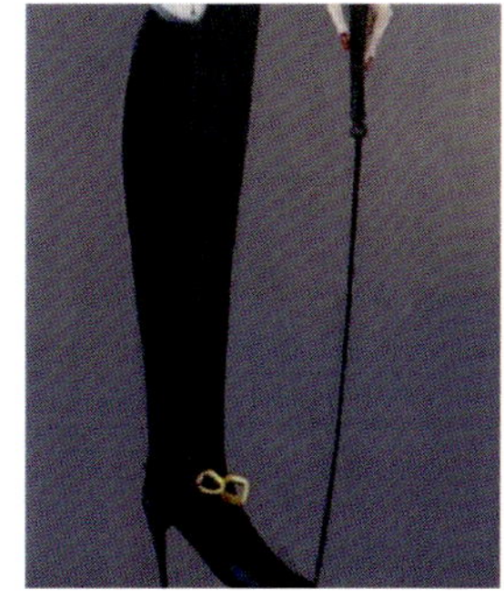

p. 20
Gold Chain 2022
Oil on Canvas
48"×36"

p. 21
Circus Affair 2024
Oil on Canvas
72"×62"

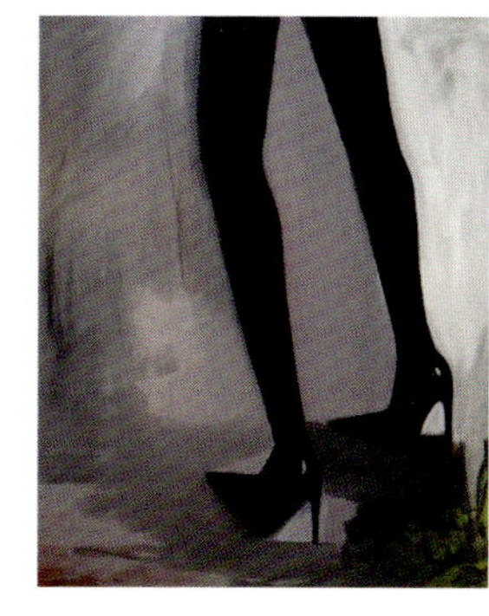

p. 22
Noir 2023
Oil on Canvas
64"×48"

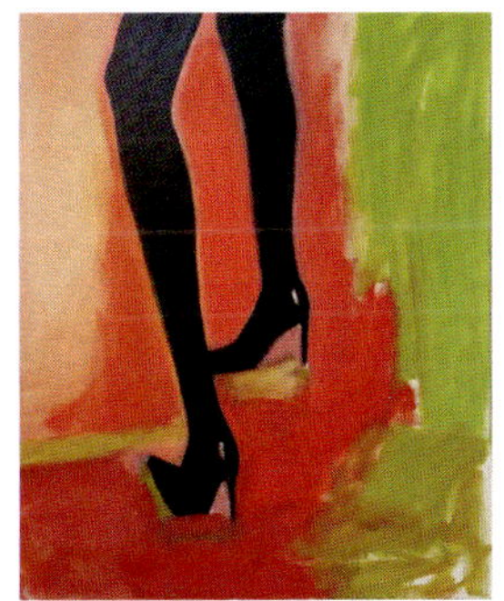

pp. 22
Heels 2023
Oil on Canvas
30"×24"

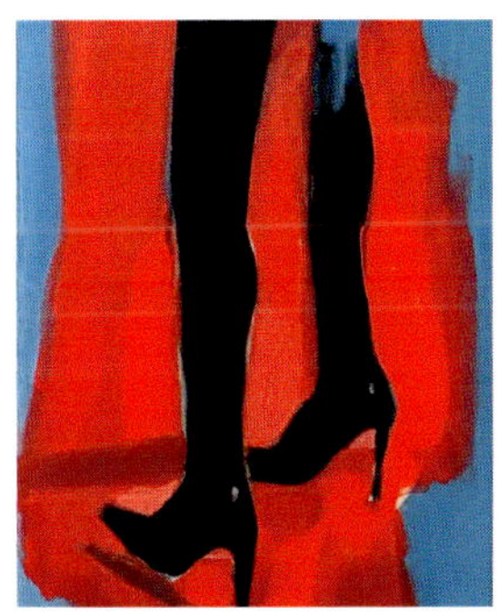

p. 23
Red Heels 2022
36"x26"

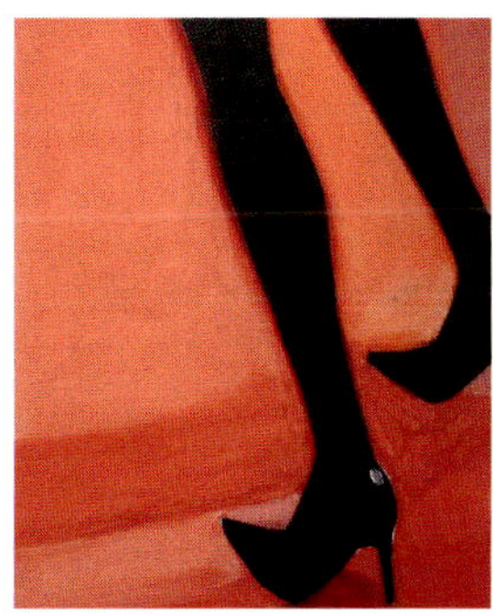

p. 24
Pink street 2023
Oil on Canvas
25"×14"

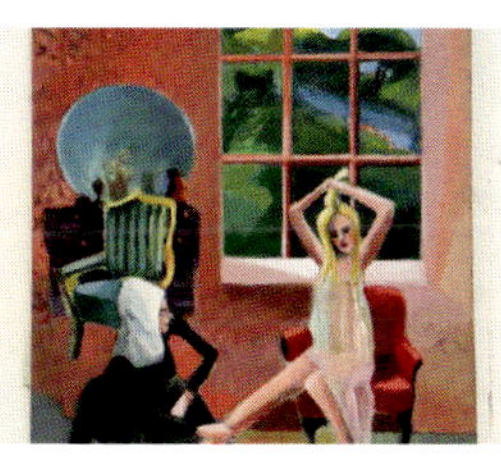

p. 25
Spring Light 2023
Oil on Canvas
48"×36"

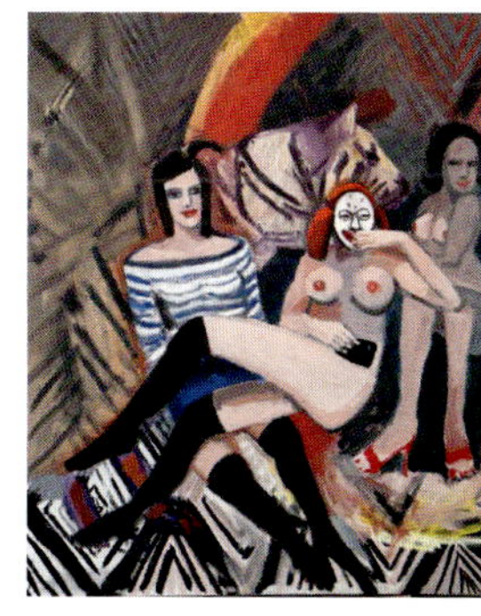

p. 26–27
Circus Affair 2024
Oil on Canvas
72"×62"

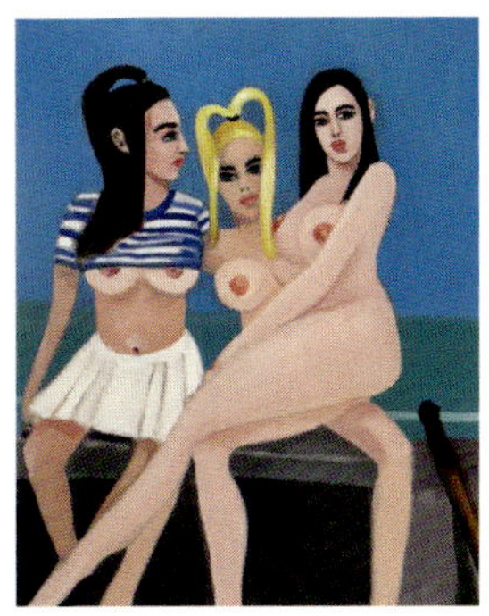

p. 28
Tennis Anyone 2024
Oil on Linen
48"×36"

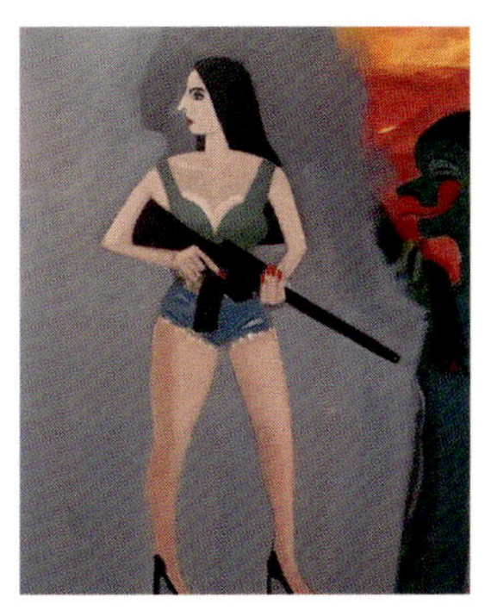

p. 29
Trigger 2023
Oil on Linen
48"×36"

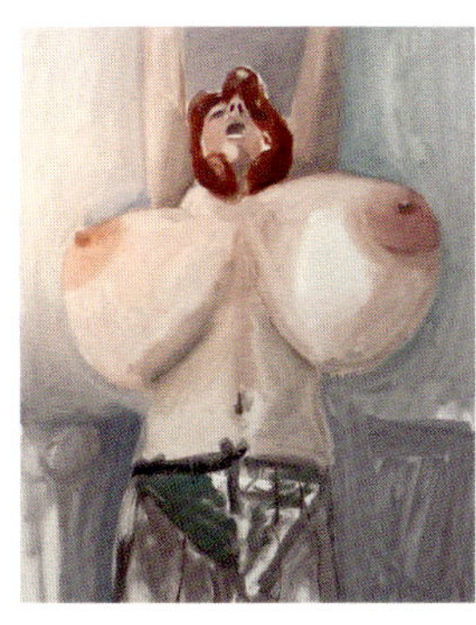

p. 30
Margaret Arms Overhead 2024
48"×38"

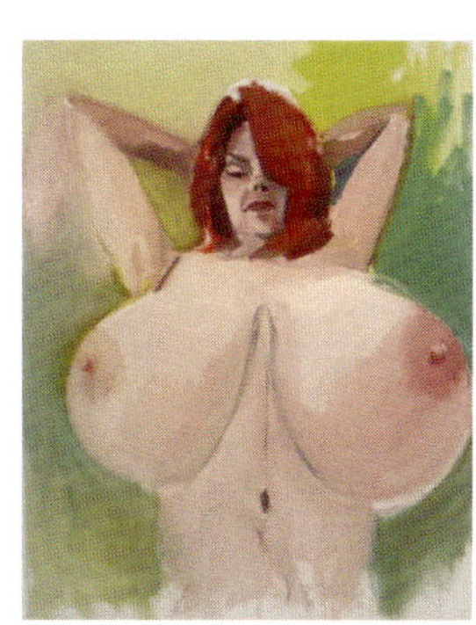

p. 31
Big Red Arms Overhead 2024
48"×38"

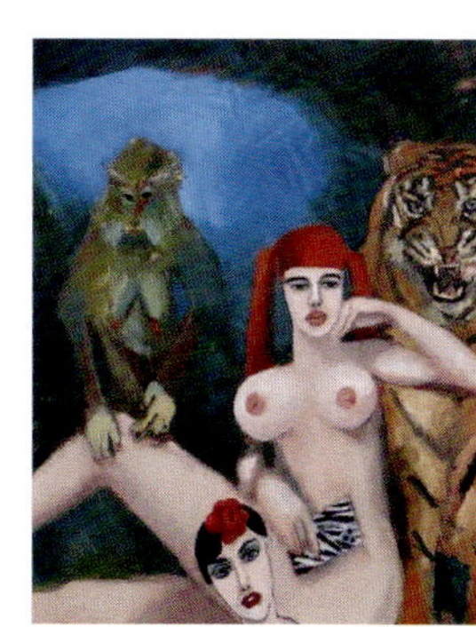

p. 32
Evolve 2023
Oil on Linen
48"×48"

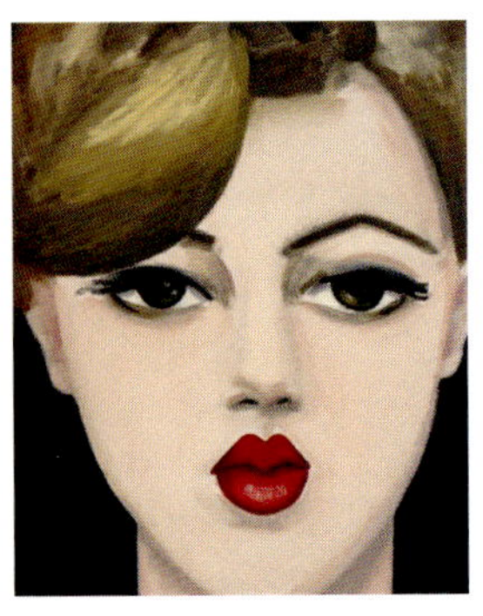

p. 33
Paris 2023
Oil on Linen
48"×36"

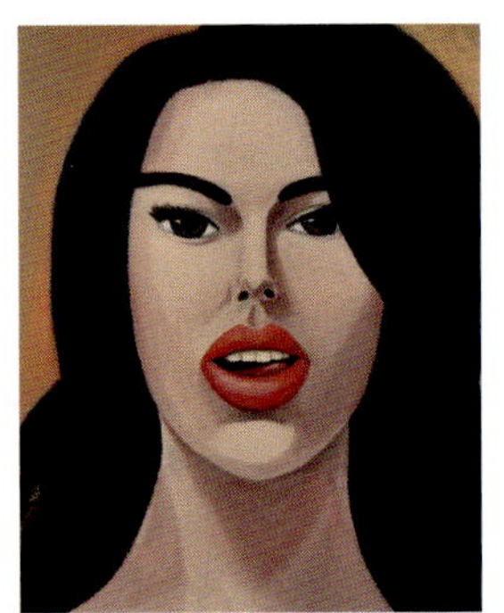

p. 34
Dalilah 2023
Oil on Canvas
64"×48"

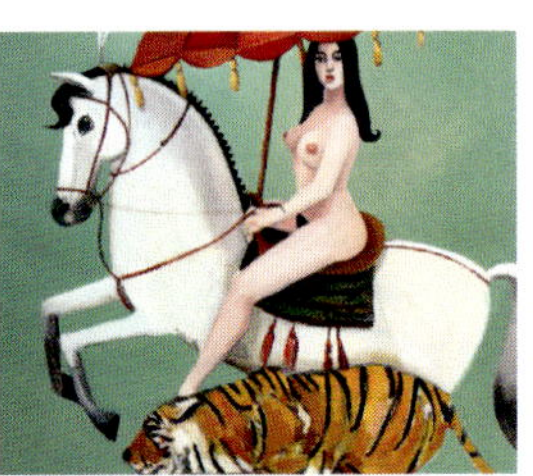

p. 35
Elope 2024
Oil on Linen
70"×70"

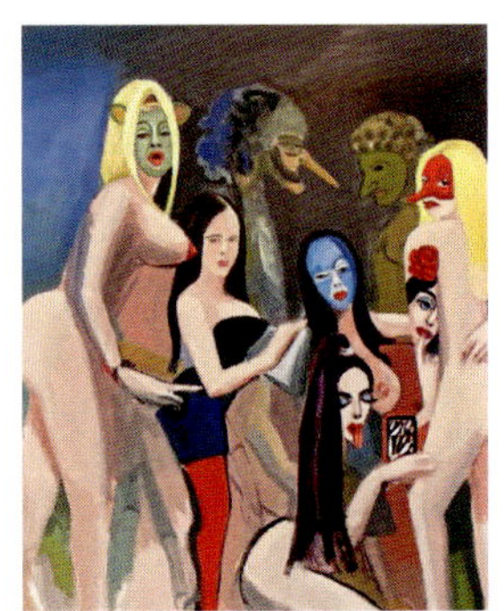

p. 36
Les Damiselle 2022
Oil on Canvas
64"×48"

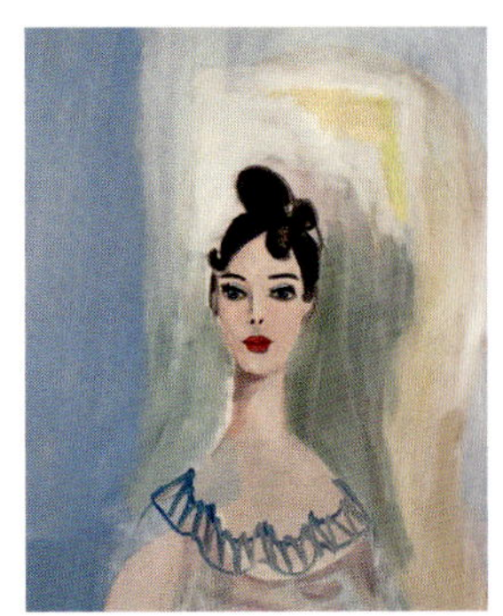

p. 37
Charlotte 2024
Oil on Linen
48"×38"

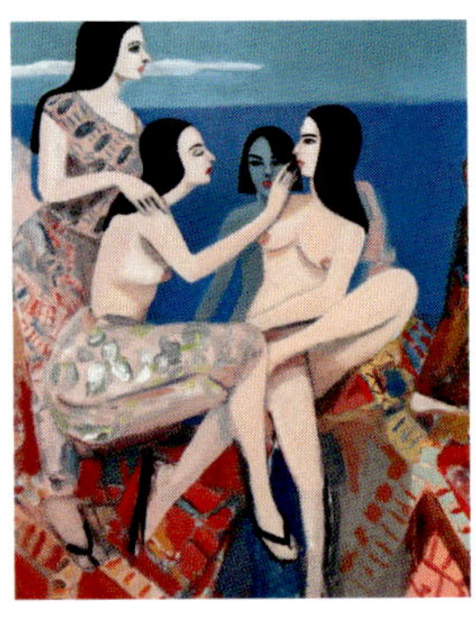

p. 38
The Beach Far Away
2024
72"×64"

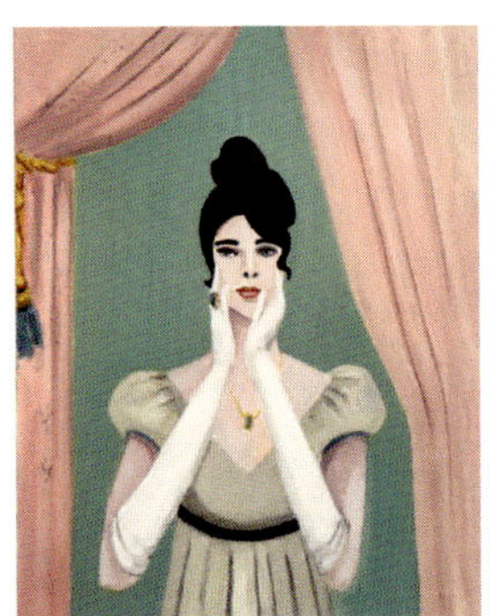

p. 39
White Gloves 2024
Oil on Linen
40"×30"

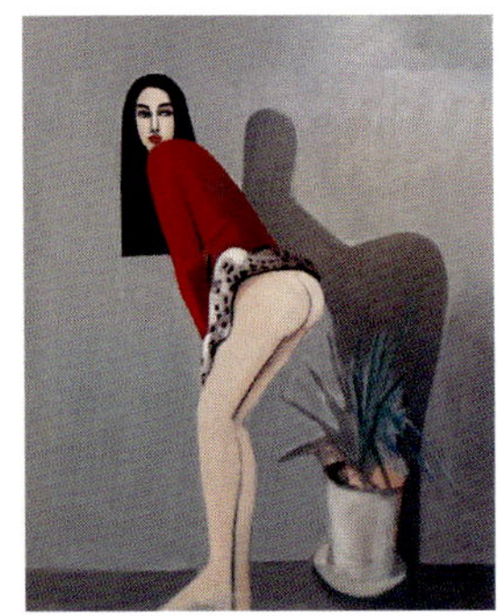

p. 40
Rear View, 2024,
Oil on Linen
48"x36"

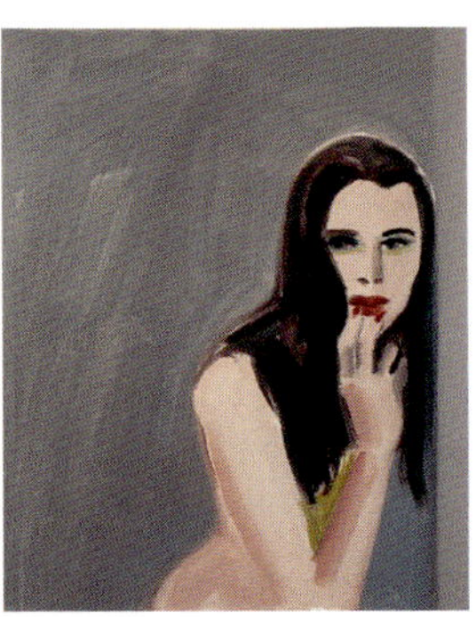

p. 41
Grey Wall 2024
Oil on Canvas
18"×16"

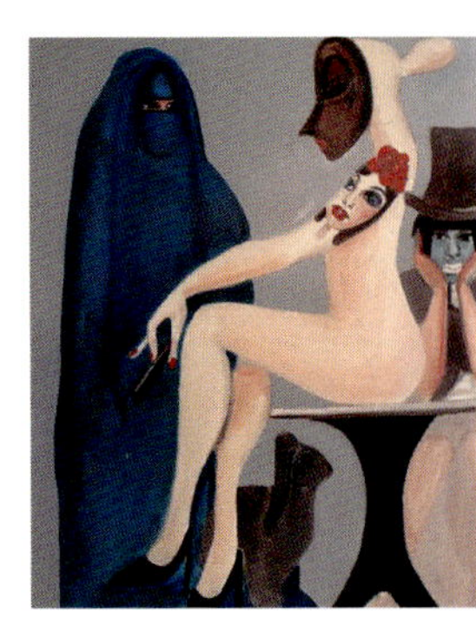

p. 42
Down The Rabbit Hole
2022
Oil on canvas
60"x40"

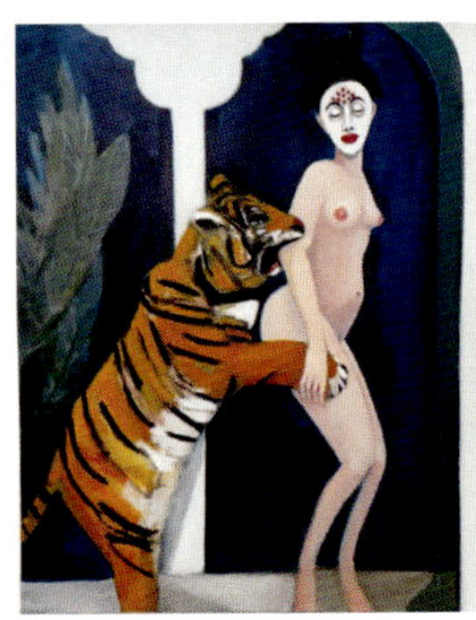

p. 43
Tiger Love 2024
Oil on Canvas
64"×48"

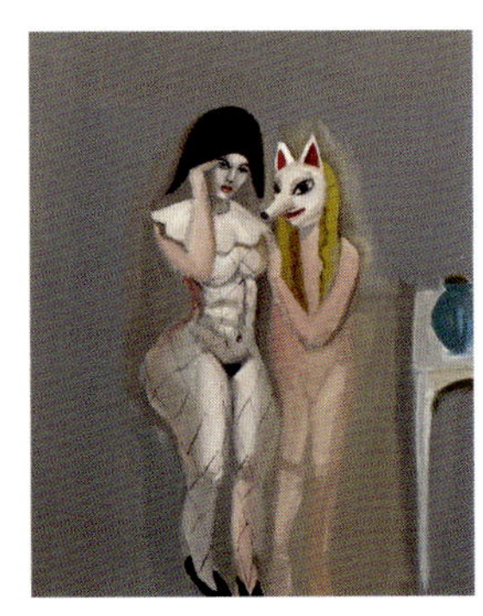

p. 44
Mother & Daughter 2024
Oil on Canvas
64"×48"

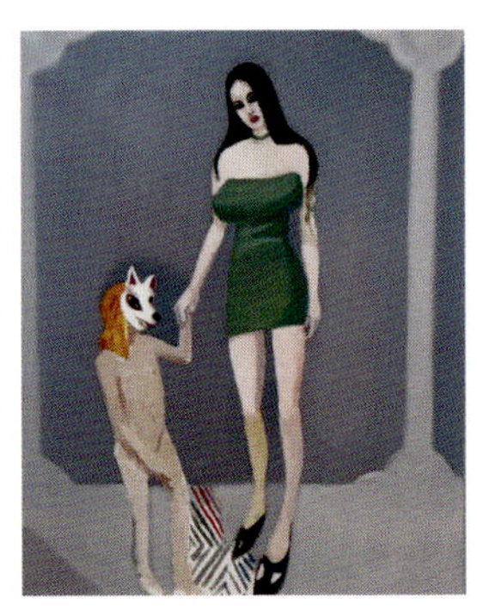

p. 45
Mother & Child 2023
Oil on Linen
48"×36"

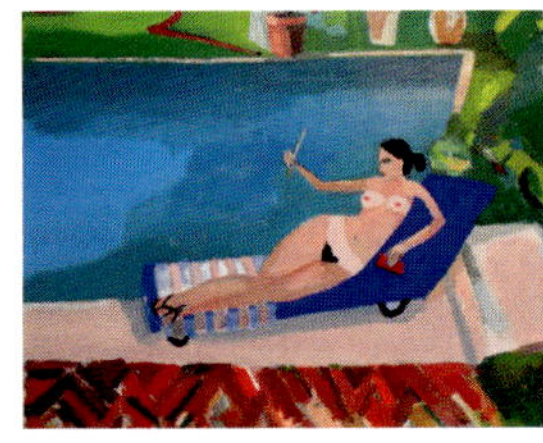

p. 46–47
Pool Side 2024
70"×70"

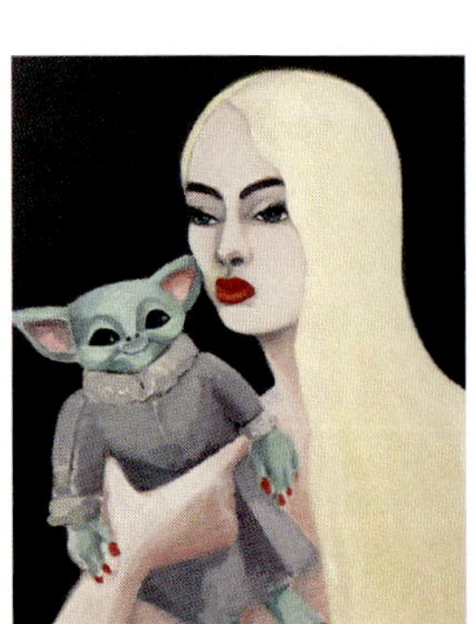

p. 48
Blonde 2022
Oil on Canvas
16"×14"